ENGLISH ❖ HERITAGE

Book of
Norwich

ENGLISH ✠ HERITAGE

Book of Norwich

Brian Ayers

B. T. Batsford Ltd/English Heritage
London

For my Mother and Father
Sheila and Vin Ayers

First published 1994

Typeset by Lasertext Ltd, Stretford, Manchester
and printed in Great Britain by
The Bath Press, Bath

Published by B T Batsford Ltd
4 Fitzhardinge Street, London W1H 0AH

A CIP catalogue record for this book is
available from the British Library

ISBN 0 7134 7568 4

Contents

Illustrations

Colour Plates

Preface

In 1698 Celia Fiennes, the celebrated traveller and journal writer, visited Norwich. She climbed the castle hill to see the whole city from its vantage point and was impressed with the view. 'It's a vast place and takes up a large tract of ground its 6 miles in compass...the whole Citty lookes like what it is, a rich thriveing industrious place.' Later, when she walked about the streets, she was shown 'a wall made of flints that are headed very finely and cut so exactly square and even, to shutt in one to another, that the whole wall is made without cement at all they say, but it appears to be very little if any mortar, it looks well very smooth shineing and black.'

These two observations, the general and the particular, but both concerned largely with the physical aspect of Norwich, illustrate the approach that I have tried to take in this book. It is a summary of the archaeology of the city, attempting to assess the development of Norwich as a city in terms of the details of its material culture. Of necessity, however, this approach needs a general historical framework upon which to hang itself. Such a framework is provided by a chronological format and reference to inescapable events such as the Norman Conquest. Nevertheless, in order that the text be not too inhibited by this need to explain the historical context, a summary table of events (p. 121) is also provided.

Norwich, a regional capital of great importance in the Middle Ages, is still one of the foremost centres of East Anglia. The main theme of this book is an assessment of how the city grew physically, socially and economically over the past millennium, studying how archaeology is helping to clarify these processes, with emphasis being placed upon the history of the city as a community peopled by citizens who had needs of food, shelter, security and spiritual nourishment.

In this way I hope that the book will be of more than local interest, for the archaeology of Norwich embodies much which is common to the experience of communities elsewhere. Norwich was an important city in the national and international economy; study of its archaeology helps to shed light on developments across much of north-western Europe. It is not, however, the intention that this book should seek continually to highlight such connections; it is foremost a summary of archaeological discovery in Norwich, not a critique of such discoveries in the context of urban development in England or northern Europe as a whole.

The archaeology of Norwich is taken to mean an all-embracing discipline, one which examines material evidence but puts it in a context provided by other forms of historical research, such as the study of topography, cartography, documents, place-names and numismatics. The book explores, therefore, how archaeological observation informs and supplements existing models of urban history.

Norwich is, to some extent, a city of superlatives. The largest walled town of any urban centre in England during the Middle Ages (larger than London and Southwark combined), it contains more surviving medieval

1 *Twelfth-century stone building excavated at St Martin-at-Palace Plain in 1981, with the church of St Martin, the Alnwick gate to the Cathedral Close and the spire of Norwich Cathedral in the background (Brian Ayers).*

churches than any town in Europe and was the richest provincial city for much of the seventeenth and eighteenth centuries, with the crowning appellation of 'Second City'. This exceptionally large city has a correspondingly diverse historic environment. It is blessed with a wealth of historic buildings, an exceptional collection of medieval documentation, a long and honourable antiquarian tradition, nationally important museums and an extraordinarily wide-ranging tradition of historical and archaeological enquiry, in both the past and the present. It would be pleasing to present this book as a synthesis of all this; regrettably that cannot be the case.

I have instead tried to give an overview of the growth of the city as seen by one who is interested in both the processes of urban development and the effects of that development. I have sought to draw on a wide variety of sources and disciplines in order to convey an impression of both the city at various periods and the different ways in which information is being gleaned.

Inevitably some aspects of both the city and the sources get short shrift. I am conscious that much more could have been written on the surviving churches or on the importance of the textile industry to the city, to cite but two examples. To have done so, however, would have created an imbalance in the book which is essentially a summary overview of the medieval and post-medieval city.

It would not have been possible to write this book at all but for the great help which I have received from friends and colleagues over the last fourteen years. Many of the ideas expressed here owe much to conversations with the late Alan Carter (formerly director of the Norwich Survey) and with Barbara Green (formerly keeper of archaeology, Norwich Castle Museum). Both of them have contributed enormously to a better understanding of the growth of the city and my debt to each is very considerable.

I owe much to other colleagues, particularly to Malcolm Atkin, Bill Milligan, Robert Smith and Margot Tillyard for providing me with informative insights into the archaeology, buildings and documentary history of Norwich. I continue to benefit also from the generosity of others who give me new information, discuss problems with me and, most importantly, point out when I am wrong! The list is long and growing but thanks must go to Nick Arber, Chris Barringer, Paul Cattermole, David Cubitt, Keith Darby, Alan Davison, Alayne Fenner, Eric Fernie, Roberta Gilchrist, Joyce Gurney-Read, Stephen Heywood, Sandy Heslop, Sarah Jennings, Derek Manning, Mary Manning, Sue Margeson, Peter Murphy, Vic Nierop-Reading, Trevor Nuthall, Andrew Rogerson and Elizabeth Rutledge. Ideas of many of these people appear in this book.

I receive great help from my colleagues in the Norfolk Archaeological Unit who give me much new information. I am especially indebted to my long-time colleague Jayne Bown, who often remembers details which I have forgotten, but also to Sarah Bates, Niall Donald, Phil Emery, Julia Huddle, Irena Lentowicz, Kenneth Penn, Jez Reeve, Andy Shelley, Liz Shepherd and Heather Wallis.

I have also received much helpful criticism from colleagues who have read either the complete text in draft or parts of it. My greatest debt is to Barbara Green who read the entire original text, made many useful comments and saved me from one or two howlers. Trevor Ashwin kindly read the prehistoric section, also saved me from howlers, and gave me useful new information. Robert Smith read and discussed with me the chapters which include details concerning the buildings of the city; again I was saved from myself. Chris Barringer read the final chapter and gently highlighted the odd startling omission. Jayne Bown, Niall Donald, Jez Reeve, Andy Shelley and Liz Shepherd have all generously provided me with useful comments on the text. My good friend Alan Browne read an early draft as a layman and gave me much useful and trenchant comment as well as ideas for the glossary. None of these individuals, of course, is responsible for any of the errors which no doubt remain.

Many of the illustrations of this book have been provided from the archives of the Norfolk Archaeological Unit with the air photographs from those of the Norfolk Landscape Archaeology Section, both organisations being part of the Field Archaeology Division of the Norfolk Joint Museums Service. The N.A.U. illustrations are as follows: 1, 10–14, 19–26, 28, 31, 35–9, 43–4, 49–52, 55–7, 60–1, 65, 68, 77, 80–1, 84 and colour photographs 2, 4 and 11. Individual N.A.U. photographers and illustrators are credited in the captions as are all other individuals and organisations who have kindly permitted illustrations to be used. Special thanks are owed to Norma Watt of the Art Department at Norwich Castle Museum for all her assistance concerning early paintings and drawings of the city. I am also most grateful to David Wicks for his assistance in providing photographs.

I am particularly in the debt of my brother David who most generously gave me a computer. This has enabled me to word process the text and has ensured not only the completion of the book but also the retention of my sanity.

Lastly I owe love and thanks to Lynn, Emily and Megan for the great forbearance and encouragement shown to me in the evening and at weekends as I have typed this work, surrounded by an inexplicable clutter of papers and books.

1

The origins and early growth of settlement

Any assessment of the archaeology of Norwich must start with the geographic setting. This is the more evident from a cursory glance at early maps of the city. Nearly all of these emphasize its location within a surrounding agricultural area. Fat sheep can be seen within and without the walls on Cuningham's plan of 1558, while cornfields and windmills are testimony to the abundance of the hinterland. The implied geographical importance of Norwich, even allowing for local propaganda, is clear.

The city stands astride the Wensum, a meandering East Anglian river which is still, although barely, tidal within the built-up area. The river enters the historic core from the north-west, its relatively wide valley becoming constricted as the stream turns eastward to pass north of the land now dominated by the Castle and Cathedral. This constriction is caused by two areas of relatively high ground, that of Mousehold Heath to the north and east, and that of the Ber Street escarpment to the south and west. East of the Cathedral, the river turns south once more and gradually the valley opens out again until it merges with that of the river Yare, into which the Wensum flows south-east of the ancient (and modern) city.

The constriction of the river valley led to the accumulation of glacial deposits, notably sands and gravels, in the valley bottom on the margins of the river. The underlying geology is chalk, with generous inclusions of flint, and is surmounted in places by Norwich crag (a Pleisto-cene deposit of a shelly sandstone). The sands and gravels can be up to seven metres (23ft) thick and form well-drained terraces, ideal for early settlement and for affording access to, and crossing of, the river.

The river was fed by tributary streams, known locally as 'cockeys', which flowed into it from either bank. The largest of these, the 'Great Cockey', occupied its own small valley to the west of the Ber Street escarpment. It rose near present-day All Saint's Green and flowed, via Red Lion Street, White Lion Street, Little London Street and School Lane, northward to the river. It was culverted by the eighteenth century but its outflow can still be seen near St George's Bridge, and damage to the culvert by modern development can lead to flooding, as occurred on Castle Street in 1962.

Other streams flowed into the river from both the north and the south banks. The largest on the north side was the Dalymond which rose in Old Catton, entered the area of the walled city at Magpie Road, formed a parish boundary as far as Magdalen Street, then flowed down at least part of Rattenrowe to enter the river at Water (now Hansard) Lane. This stream was observed still running during a watching brief off Rattenrowe in 1985.

The location of these streams clearly had an effect upon early settlement. They provided water for domestic and industrial purposes but they also defined areas of the developing community. It will be seen that the alignment

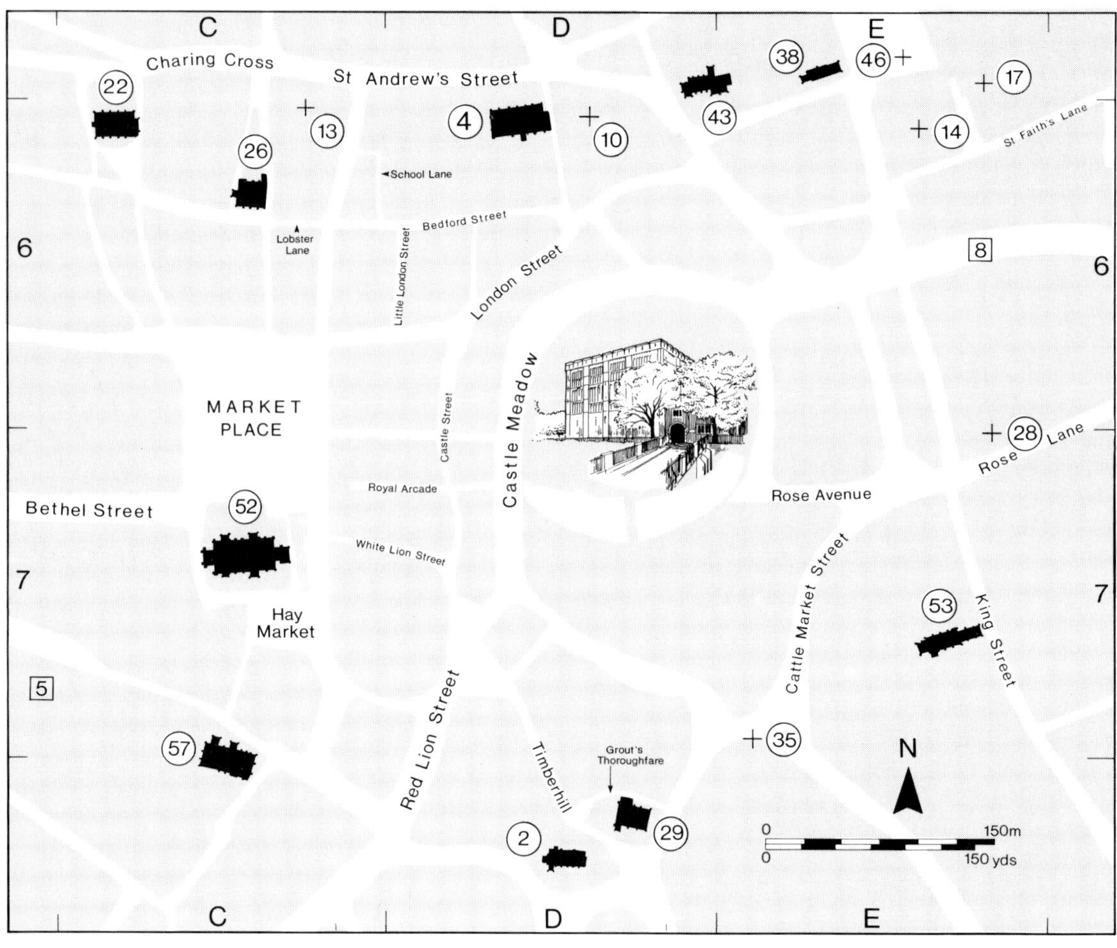

Above is detail of central area opposite.

Key to Churches and Religious Houses
Churches are represented by a circle, Religious Houses by a square.

○ CHURCHES

1	All Saints Fyebriggate
2	All Saints Westlegate
3	Christ Church
	Holy Trinity
4	St Andrew
5	St Augustine
6	St Bartholomew
7	St Benedict
8	St Botolph
9	St Catherine
10	St Christopher
11	St Clement Colegate
12	St Clement Conesford
13	St Crouche
14	St Cuthbert
15	St Edmund
16	St Edward
17	St Ethelbert
18	St Etheldreda
19	St George Colegate
20	St George Tombland
21	St Giles
22	St Gregory
23	St Helen
24	St James
25	St John de Sepulchre
26	St John Maddermarket
27	St John the Baptist
28	St John the Evangelist
29	St John Timberhill
30	St Julian
31	St Laurence
32	St Margaret in combusto
33	St Margaret Newbridge
34	St Margaret Westwick
35	St Martin in Balliva
36	St Martin-at-Oak
37	St Martin-at-Palace
38	St Mary the Less
39	St Mary Combuste
40	St Mary Coslany
41	St Mary-in-the-Marsh
42	St Mathew
43	St Michael at Pleas
44	St Michael Conesford
45	St Michael Coslany
46	St Michael Tombland
47	St Michael-at-Thorn
48	St Olaf Conesford
49	St Olave Pitt Street
50	St Paul
51	St Peter Hungate
52	St Peter Mancroft
53	St Peter Parmentergate
54	St Peter Southgate
55	St Saviour
56	SS Simon and Jude
57	St Stephen
58	St Swithin
59	St Vedast
60	St Anne

□ RELIGIOUS HOUSES

1	Augustinian Friary
2	Carmelite Friary
3	Carrow Priory
4	Cathedral Priory
5	College of St Mary in the Fields
6	Dominican Friary (first site)
7	Dominican Friary (second site)
8	Franciscan Friary
9	Great Hospital
10	Hildebrond's Hospital
11	Lazar House
12	Norman Hospital
13	St Leonard's Priory
14	St Michael's Chapel
15	St William's Chapel

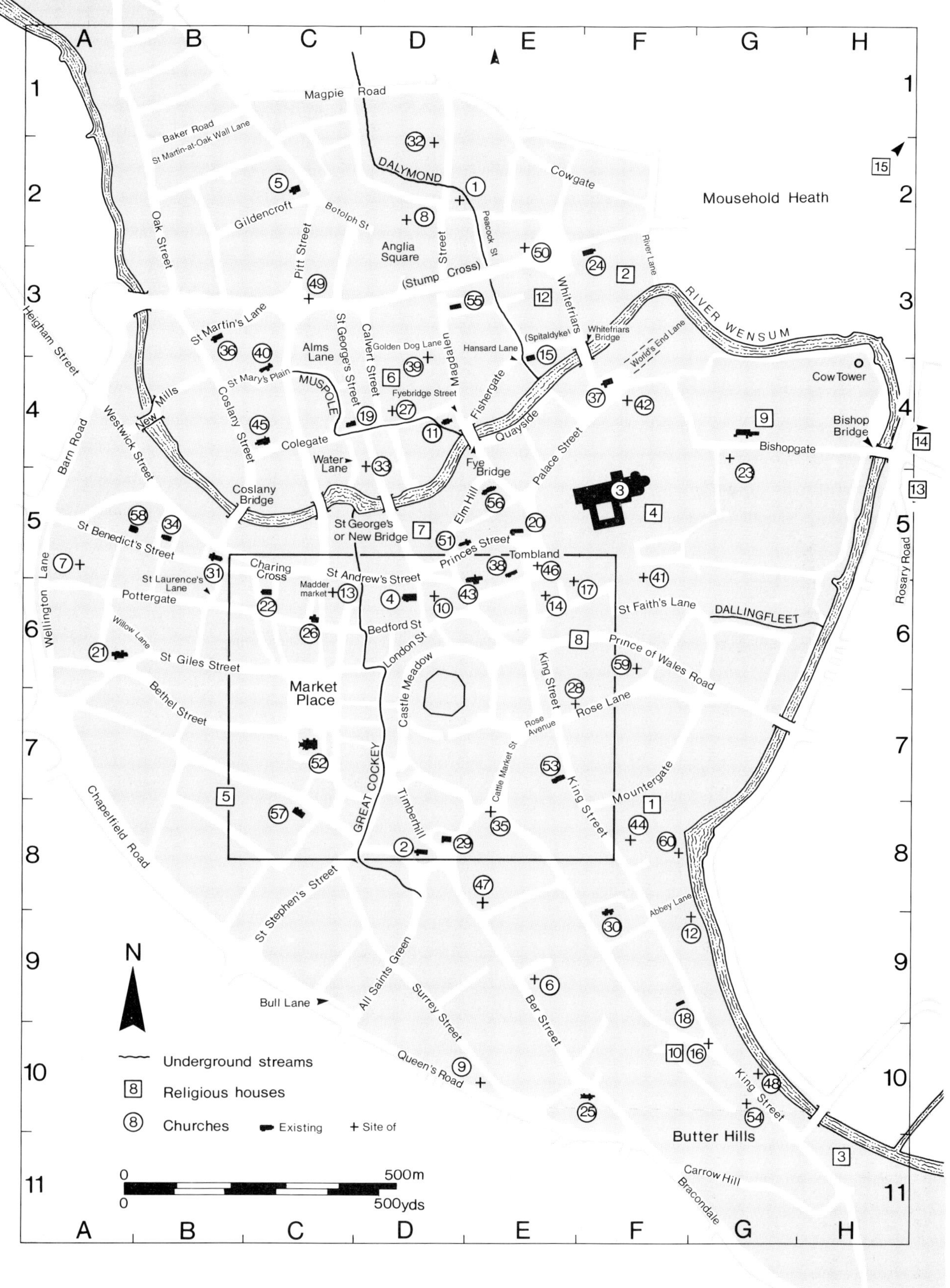

2. *Plan of Norwich within the walls showing street-names mentioned in the text* (Karen Guffogg).

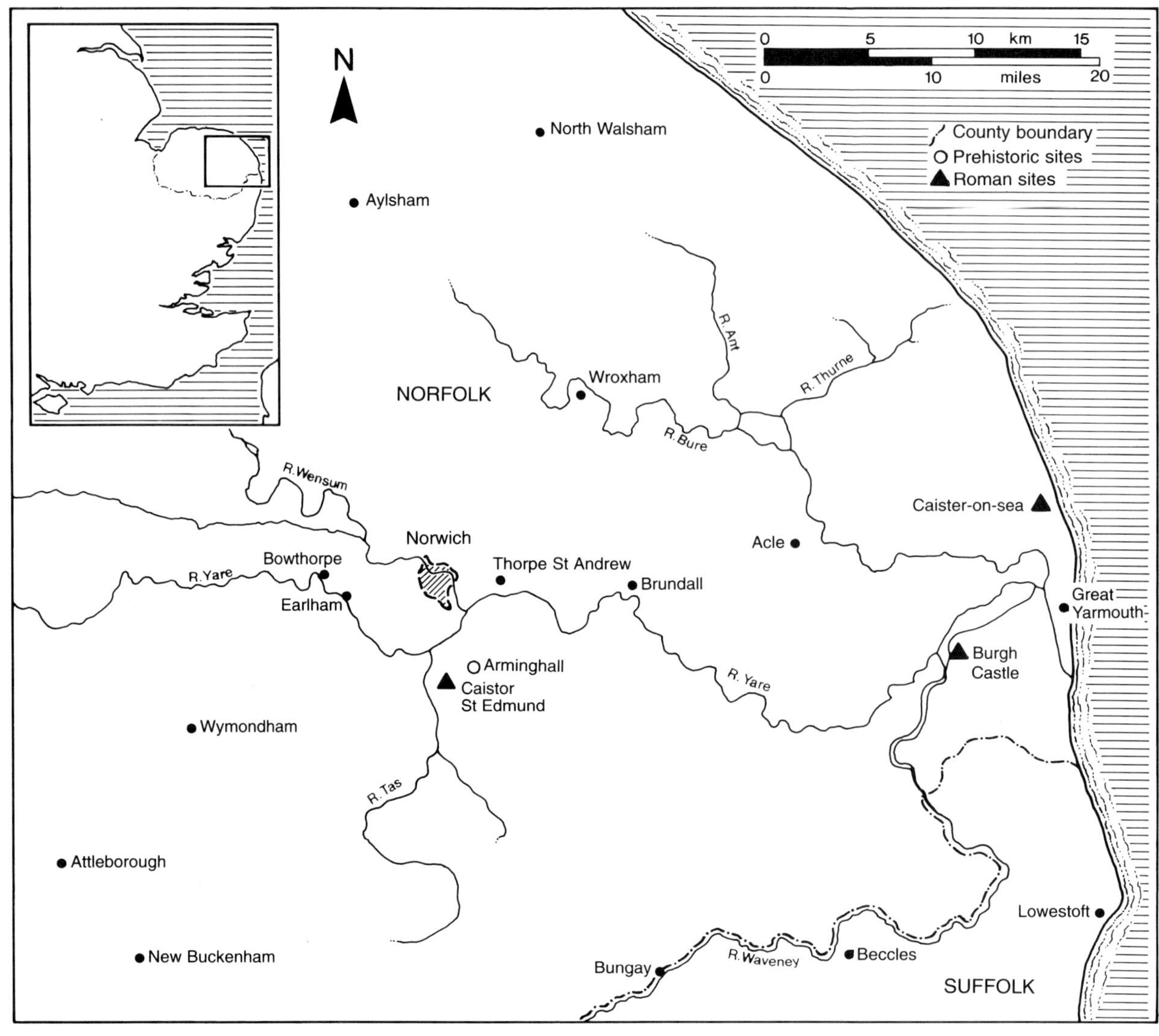

3 Map of Norwich in its region (Karen Guffogg).

of certain streets and boundaries is due to the presence of such tributaries. An important aspect of archaeological work continues to be the attempt to reconstruct the alignments and nature of these geographical features and their small valleys, the masking of which in recent centuries has obscured the early topography of the city. The steep hills to the south and north-east, together with the cockey valleys, present a landscape which belies the popular notion of Norfolk as 'very flat'. Norwich is indeed one of the hilliest cities in England and current investigation is beginning to indicate that it was originally hillier still (**4**). Work in both the valley of the Great Cockey and near the outflow of the Muspole (on the north bank) has shown that infilling has flattened out the natural topography.

The hillslopes and gravel terraces on either bank of the river, while good for settlement, are not necessarily ideal areas for the archaeologist. Most of Norwich is well-drained, with moisture running off through the gravels and chalk. This inhibits the development of waterlogged

4 *Steps at the east end of St Laurence's church, connecting Westwick Street with St Benedict's Street and illustrating the unexpected hilliness of Norwich topography* (Brian Ayers).

anaerobic deposits and the preservation of organic materials on archaeological sites in the city is generally poor. Such deposits only exist at the river margins.

The building stone of the city is also poor. There are no local supplies of good quality freestone or, indeed, of any freestone. In consequence most buildings were constructed for many centuries in timber or flint with a chalk and flint rubble wall core. Freestone dressings were expensive and thus tended to be robbed from disused buildings. Archaeological interpretation can be impeded when an excavated wall footing consists solely of flint rubble with its distinctive dressings missing. Archaeological evidence is therefore often hard-won, the more so in that much of the city has been occupied intensively for a millennium. Conversely, however, the existence of slopes and the resulting

attempts to level or reduce these can often lead to situations where deposits and features are remarkably well-preserved due to deliberate burial.

Norwich, like other important East Anglian towns such as Ipswich and Thetford, is not Roman in origin but grew to prominence in the Anglo-Saxon period. The settlement's name does not appear in any known document before the 980s; the earliest map is a sketch of about 1540 and the earliest illustrations of topographical use also date from the sixteenth century. It follows that the evidence of the urban topography and archaeology, supported by allied disciplines such as place-name study and numismatics, provides the only key to an understanding of origins and early growth.

Pre-urban settlement

It will become clear that those settlements which were eventually to form the nucleus of the modern city appear to date from the mid to late seventeenth century. The area of medieval and modern Norwich, however, masks an environment which has been settled in one form or another since prehistoric times. The archaeology of the pre-urban environment is as much a part of the history of Norwich as the development of the city itself.

Palaeolithic (*c.* 500,000–10,000 BC) and mesolithic (*c.* 10,000–4500 BC) material is naturally sparse. Palaeolithic flints, including a handaxe, were reported from Mousehold Heath in 1935 and 1974, while handaxes and flakes were recovered at Carrow, immediately south of the medieval city wall in 1927–8 and 1963. Large numbers of palaeolithic flints were recovered from gravel pits in Whitlingham Marsh in the 1920s. Flakes now thought to be mesolithic were reported from Carrow (in 1887), from the top of Carrow Hill (before 1947) and at Boundary Road (in 1964).

None of these finds was located in the historic centre of the medieval city, although a blade of possible mesolithic date was found at the corner of Cowgate and Magdalen Street in

17

5 *Air photograph of the Arminghall Henge (*Derek Edwards, Norfolk Landscape Archaeology*)*.

1974. Excavation in 1985, however, on Fishergate next to the river Wensum, uncovered a thick peat deposit above the river gravels. Environmental evidence, together with radiocarbon dating, of the lower levels of this peat indicated that the mesolithic valley in about 7000 BC was wooded and suitable for human occupation.

Early neolithic finds (*c.* 4500–2500 BC) in the greater Norwich area are almost as sparse as those of palaeolithic and mesolithic date but later neolithic (*c.* 2500–2000 BC) and Bronze Age (*c.* 2000–800 BC) activity is becoming increasingly notable in the archaeological record. Stray flint finds are recorded from a number of city-centre sites, such as King Street (before 1898), at the site of the City Hall (in 1935) and dredged from the river Wensum (in 1950). The bulk of recorded evidence, however, comes from the greater area of modern Norwich and particularly from the river valleys and hills to the south of the city.

Here, a nationally important neolithic monument survives as a buried archaeological feature. This is the Arminghall Henge, a monument similar to the more famous henges of Wessex, but constructed of wood (**5**). It lies in the Yare valley a short distance above its confluence with the Wensum and was appar-

ently a ceremonial monument, being first observed from the air in the 1920s and partially excavated in the 1930s. Henges are often found at river confluences in eastern England.

The Arminghall Henge is merely the most important prehistoric monument in one of the most archaeologically rich areas of Norfolk. It is surrounded by sites of late prehistoric, Romano-British and medieval date. Some survive as field monuments; others are known from antiquarian observations (as when Markshall cemetery was largely destroyed for a railway cutting); many have been plotted by field survey, many others by air photography.

The predominant archaeological feature is the ring-ditch or ploughed-out barrow, and air photography has now identified a considerable number of these. Some have been excavated, the most comprehensive series of excavations being those which preceded construction of the

6 *Excavation of prehistoric ring-ditches and a seventh-century Saxon cemetery at Harford Farm, Norwich Southern Bypass 1989 (*Derek Edwards, Norfolk Landscape Archaeology*)*.

Norwich Southern Bypass (1989–90). Early Bronze Age ring-ditches were sampled at Bixley while five flattened barrows, including two of elaborate 'disc' type, were excavated at Harford Farm (**6**). Earlier excavation had sampled barrows on Eaton Heath in the 1820s, a complex ring-ditch at Bowthorpe west of the city was excavated in 1979 (where a central burial was augmented by ten supplementary burials) and a ring-ditch at Sweet Briar Road northwest of the city was uncovered in 1982.

These Bronze Age monuments were all located in areas away from the historic core of Norwich, where only occasional finds of archaeological material hint at Bronze Age activity (such as the discovery of a barbed-and-tanged arrowhead in 1979 on the site of the Anglia Television offices). Bronze Age metalwork, however, is known from the area south and west of the city with finds reported from Unthank Road, Peckover Road and Eaton.

South of the city, the Harford Farm excavations uncovered at least six square-ditched enclosures which may date from the Iron Age. Five silver Icenian coins were found before 1940 in the vicinity of Weston Road and Iron Age material is also known from the village of Trowse, just south of the medieval city.

Roman finds from Norwich are much more common. This is not, however, as a result of intensive Roman occupation, but largely through the reuse of Roman material in later centuries, much of it probably being pillaged from the important Roman settlement of *Venta Icenorum* or Caistor St Edmund some 5km (3 miles) south of the city (**7**). This much may be commemorated by the ancient doggerel couplet:

> Caistor was a city when Norwich was none
> Norwich was built with Caistor's stone

Caistor Roman town stands in the valley of the Tas, a tributary of the Yare, and dates from the first century with walls being added in the third. The site is now an open field (with a church in the south-east corner). The forum

7 Venta Icenorum *(Caistor St Edmund Roman town) from the air (© Crown Copyright/MOD).*

area and two *insulae* were excavated in the 1930s as was the south gate where a substantial masonry structure was located.

The hinterland of Caistor is also rich in Roman sites, notably that of a temple to the north-east, and the settlement was naturally served by roads, one of which probably ran northwards to cross the river Yare close to the present Lakenham Bridge before climbing Long John Hill to the Ber Street ridge which separates the Yare and Wensum valleys (**8**). Here the road lay within the area of the later medieval core of Norwich and seems to have continued northward to a crossing of the Wensum at the southern end of Oak Street. It followed Oak Street to the line of the present-day Aylsham Road. An alternative alignment has been suggested along the river Wensum, following present-day King Street.

A north to south Roman road on either alignment would have been crossed by an east to west road (which has been given the name Holmestreet Way). This second road ran from a probable Roman port at Brundall, situated on the river Yare to the east of Norwich, entered the area of the modern city at Pilling Park, crossed the river Wensum by means of a ford at Bishop Bridge, proceeded westward along a causeway which is now Bishopgate, passed through the site of the later Cathedral (probably on the line of the nave), ran westward

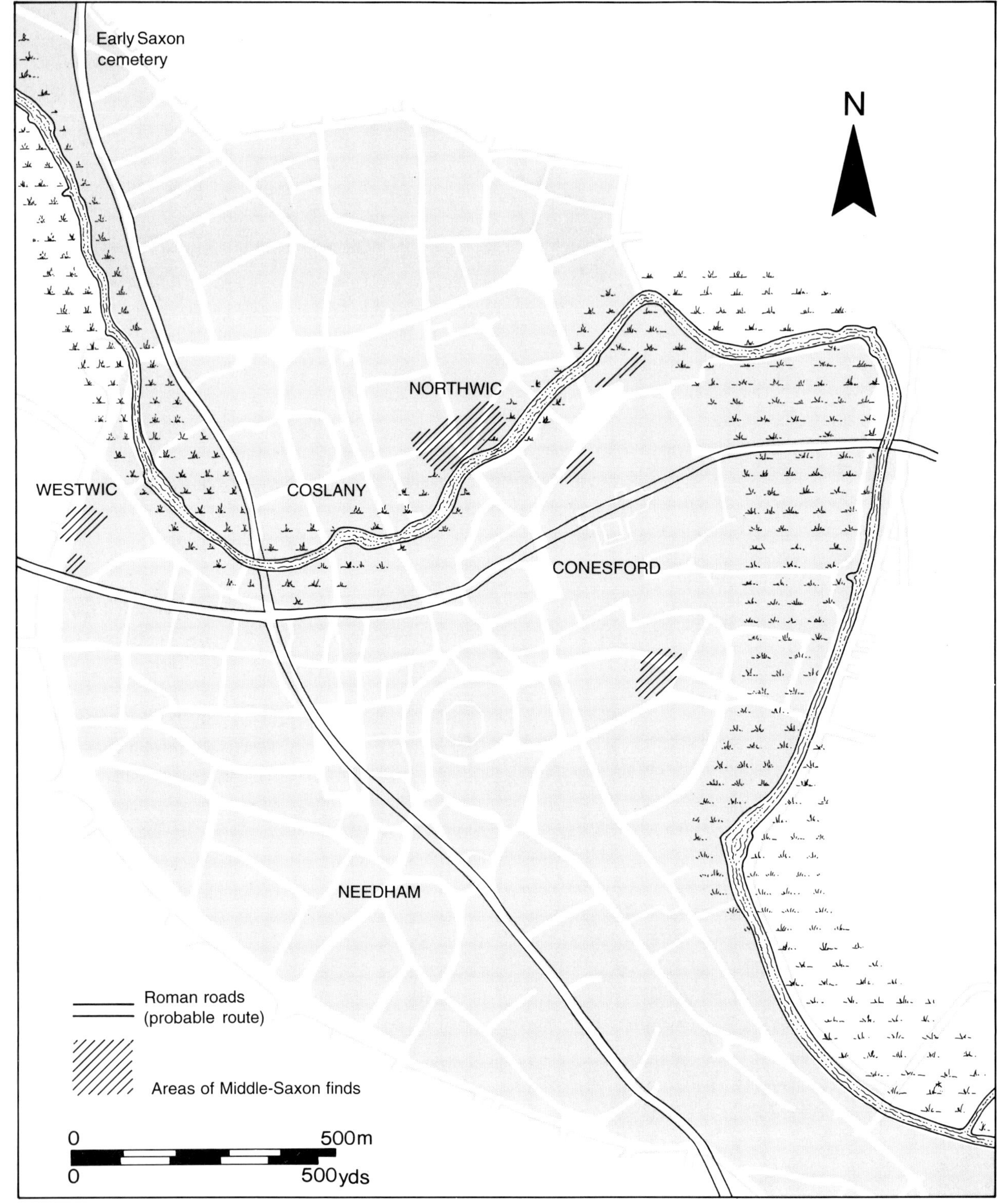

8 *Map showing probable alignments of Roman roads, Middle Saxon place-names and find spots of Middle Saxon material in the area of the later medieval city (*Karen Guffogg*).*

along St Benedict's Street before leaving the area of the city via the Dereham Road. The Bishopgate causeway would have been necessary to keep the road out of the marsh and its existence seems to have been confirmed recently by structural problems in a Bishopgate house whose footings apparently straddle the causeway edge.

The probable alignment of these Roman roads indicates that the geographical importance of Norwich was recognized in the Roman period, even if not exploited by settlement. The crossing point on the Wensum of Holmestreet Way is the lowest ford on the river and, once bridged (probably in the thirteenth century), remained the lowest bridging point on the Wensum and Yare until the construction of the Haven Bridge at Great Yarmouth in the sixteenth century. It is possible, however, that there was a further crossing downstream of the modern city in the Roman period. Commercial excavations in 1961, some 30m (100ft) below the confluence of the Wensum and Yare, located a timber platform some 3.8m (12ft) below the level of the modern marsh, which may have formed a wharf or bridgehead.

Roman finds within Norwich, however, do not indicate settlement of any density, although pottery finds in 1974 and 1987 on sites adjacent to Magdalen Street suggest the possibility of a farmstead north of the river. A barrow, which once lay on meadows where Thorpe Railway Station now stands, may also have been Romano-British in date. It was opened about 1826 by Woodward, who thought it 'Danish', and contained 'urns of rude workmanship' as well as cremated bone.

This presumed Roman barrow, immediately east of the medieval city, was supplemented by further discoveries some 2km (1¼ miles) further east in 1950. Construction of a tennis court at Stanley Avenue revealed two cremation burials of first-century date with rich grave goods. The first contained a handled flagon, a platter with cremated bones, a white bronze mirror with a wooden mirror case, a blue glass bead and

three coins of Nero. The second burial also contained a handled flagon and a platter with fragments of a jar and the remains of a bronze pin. Roman burial finds remain rare throughout Norfolk and these discoveries at Stanley Avenue thus have a significance considerably greater than their number.

A burial found at Woodlands Park, Dereham Road, in 1861 was reported by one John Wodderspoon to his friend T. Barton in a letter dated 10 December of that year. After thanking Barton for a brace of pheasants, he went on to say that he had

> a few waifs and strays for you in the Archaeological line.... You saw of course that workmen found what I believe to be a Roman interment in lead...the body was either a youth or female – the teeth, some of which I brought away, very beautiful....

It is likely that the discovery was third or fourth century in date. It consisted of a female skeleton in an unsoldered lead coffin with remains of another skeleton close by. Both the Stanley Avenue and Dereham Road discoveries were close to Holmestreet Way.

Other than these burials, evidence for Romano-British occupation is sparse, unlike that for the reuse of Roman material, much of it probably from Caistor. Roman bricks are built into the fabric of the Norman Cathedral, while probable Romano-British rotary querns were discovered in 1948 reused as building materials for eighteenth-century houses above the city ditch at Barn Road. Pottery sherds and coins are found scattered throughout the city, including coins of Claudius II, Aurelian and Diocletian from the corner of Dove Street and the Market Place, close to the probable line of the north to south Roman road. Such finds often cause problems of interpretation; it is likely that some of the exotic Roman coinage from the city arrived as souvenirs brought by men of the Royal Norfolk Regiment in the nineteenth century.

Compared to a Roman settlement site, however, the material from Norwich is scanty. Evidence for the centuries immediately succeeding the Roman period is also thin. A pagan Saxon cremation cemetery of fifth- to sixth-century date was discovered at Eade Road, north of the later city wall, in about May 1898. A man named Pike recovered an urn reputedly of fifth-century type and fragments of others; further finds, including a square-headed brooch, were found in July the same year. Apart from the brooch (which passed to the Castle Museum), the discoveries were dispersed (the urn going to the British Museum).

A fragment of cremation urn was also recovered in the early 1970s during underpinning of the chancel wall of the church of St Michael at Pleas in the heart of the city. Although isolated, this discovery is of interest given the later importance of the church as a leet court and possible moot. A few similar sherds are also known from the area of the Norwich School within the Cathedral Close.

None of this amounts to sufficient evidence to suggest that any activity before the eighth century (at the earliest) can be regarded as 'proto-urban' (that is, a precursor to the establishment of the town). Recently, excavation at Harford Farm, south of the city on the line of the Southern Bypass (1989–90), uncovered a graveyard of probable seventh-century date with grave goods which probably reflect an increasing level of affluence within the Norwich area. The discoveries were made on the hill overlooking the site of Caistor Roman town to the south and the later medieval city of Norwich to the north. The cemetery may represent part of a gradual shift in emphasis northwards, away from the Yare–Tas valley and towards the Wensum–Yare valley but it does not present evidence for an early urban existence.

Middle Saxon occupation

It is not until the eighth century that it becomes possible to suggest that pre-urban settlements were beginning to appear in the Wensum valley. These probably formed the earliest

9 *Excavation through the City Wall at Barn Road in 1952; the figure is Peter Gathercole who supervised the work. He is crouching on the inside of the wall (provenance unknown).*

nuclei of the area that became the medieval city. The evidence for even these, however, remains sparse. It has therefore been a major objective of recent work to make this evidence less equivocal, and rough patterns of occupation are beginning to emerge.

Archaeological work concentrated initially upon the plotting of finds, predominantly those of pottery fragments but also of other artefacts, in order to produce distribution maps of eighth-century Middle Saxon material from across the city. While such maps are necessarily subject to variables (for instance, nearly all of the material was located in 'secondary' contexts; that is it had been dumped within landfill or otherwise disturbed, rather than discarded where it was used) it does become possible to suggest areas of the city where concentrations of finds occur.

These areas were compared with place-name evidence as many early street and other names in Norwich can be shown to be Middle Saxon in origin. Examples include Westwick (as in Westwick Street), Coslany (as in St Michael Coslany), Conesford (Anglo-Scandinavian but based on an earlier formation and used in Conesford – now King – Street) and even Northwic (or Norwich). From here it was possible to predict probable areas of settlement and draw up a hypothetical model of the earliest settlement pattern which could then be tested by excavation and watching briefs.

The work is still in its relatively early stages and the information currently available is such that two different hypotheses of early urban growth can be postulated. The first of these is the 'nucleated' hypothesis which envisages a number of small discrete settlements, the possible areas of which are determined by the distribution of Middle Saxon material and the juxtaposition of early place-names. This has resulted in the gradual evolution of a number of maps indicating such settlements on both banks of the river Wensum.

Using this 'nucleated' model, it is possible to envisage 'Westwick', for instance, as lying in the westernmost part of the later, medieval city, close to the south bank of the river Wensum. Pottery located in excavations at Barn Road in 1952 was the first of Middle Saxon date to be found in Norwich (**9**). Occupation could have extended westward along Heigham Street (although there is little evidence for this yet) but probably did not extend to the east (modern Westwick Street being the road to Westwick rather than the road within it).

A nucleated 'Coslany' would have stood at the southern end of Oak Street on the north bank. Two churches, St Michael (or Miles) and St Mary are of apparent but undocumented early origin. 'Conesford' could have been located in the area now occupied by the northern part of the Cathedral Close, perhaps confined to an area largely north of the Holme-street Roman road. A fourth settlement,

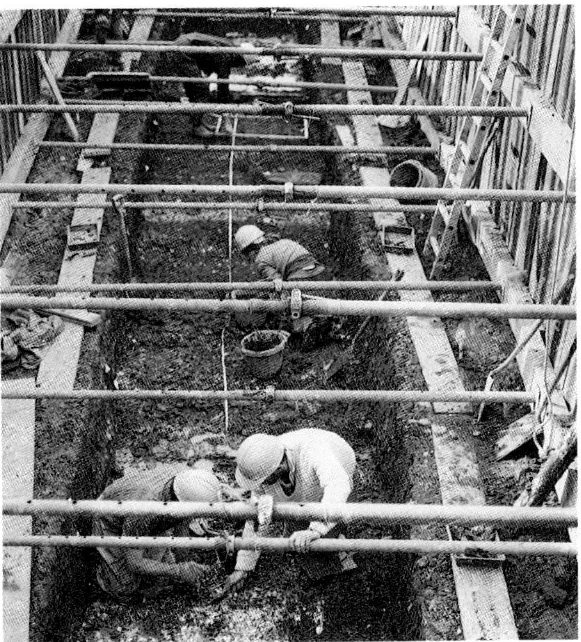

10 *Excavations on Fishergate in 1985 immediately north of the river Wensum (Brian Ayers).*

'Needham', was thought to lie where the Castle precinct now stands, but massive excavations in 1989–91 failed to locate any evidence and this settlement, if it existed ('Needham' could merely refer to a 'poor meadow'), probably lay further to the west, possibly within the small river valley of the Great Cockey stream (Needham Slough was a boggy area in this valley).

'Northwic' is the most difficult settlement to locate within the hypothesis as it eventually gave its name to the whole area of the city. Some commentators maintain that it would have been synonymous with Conesford and therefore stood somewhere in the vicinity of the Cathedral Close; recent work, however, would suggest that a more probable location lay to the north of the river. If so, it was probably, from the outset, the largest and the most important of the settlements.

Evidence for this assertion was provided by excavations on Fishergate in 1985 (**10**). These recovered considerable quantities of pottery sherds and other artefacts of Middle Saxon date (**11**). While low compared to early towns

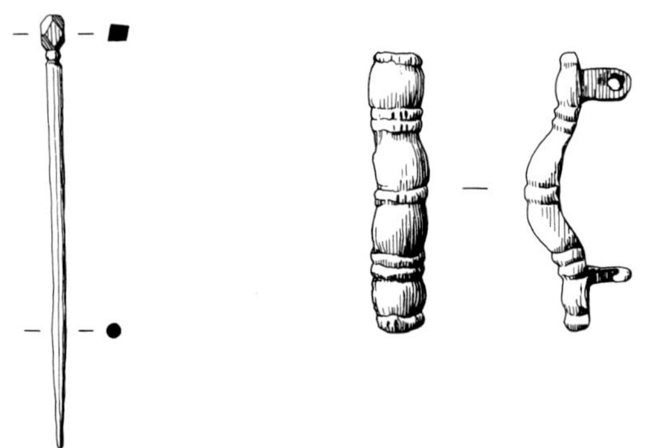

11 *Middle Saxon pin and caterpillar brooch from excavations on Fishergate, 1985 (*Jean Stokes*).*

such as Ipswich (and many field-walked rural sites), the total of over 160 sherds is large in a Norwich context. The excavation produced more Middle Saxon material than all the previous excavations in the city combined. The deposits from which the finds were recovered were secondary, being rubbish infill next to the river, but they must represent the cleansing of occupation areas nearby.

More recent discoveries of Middle Saxon pottery off Rose Lane, however, have led to the establishment of a second hypothesis. This moves away from the idea of localized nucleated settlements and towards the concept of a more traditional form of early occupation. It envisages the colonization of the river margins in an extended ribbon development. The distribution of Middle Saxon material throughout the city is marked by the concentration of discoveries close to the river on both banks. It is notable that the greatest concentrations of pottery (from Fishergate, Barn Road and Rose Lane) are all from riverine sites while the major place-names (Northwic, Westwic, Conesford and Coslany) can all be associated with the river or with river crossings.

Such ribbon development would not preclude the growth of one area as a more important part of overall settlement. Topographically, the area north of the river either side of Fyebridge Street (and including Fishergate) can be suggested as the most likely location for such a nucleus. Unfortunately, it

is also an area which has received very little archaeological attention. This is partly due to a lack of redevelopment in recent years as most rebuilding took place either before or shortly after the Second World War. There is sufficient general evidence, however, to postulate early significance.

Fishergate itself runs eastward from Fyebridge Street, the latter named from the most important medieval river crossing and possibly reflecting an earlier Roman crossing. West of Fyebridge Street is a further street, Colegate, which extends, like Fishergate, along the north bank of the river. Both Fishergate and Colegate run towards streams (the Dalymond and the Muspole respectively) which could have acted as boundaries for nascent settlement. Early documentary references to the Spitaldike, immediately east of the Dalymond and north of the eastern arm of Fishergate, refer to it as the boundary of the borough.

Fyebridge Street runs northward (as Magdalen Street) towards Stump Cross, a fork in the road lost since construction of the Inner Ring Road in 1974 (the area immediately north of this was known by the early name of *Mereholt* – 'boundary wood'). Listed buildings line both sides of Magdalen Street (as on much of Colegate) and it has thus remained largely immune to archaeological excavation. The potential of this main axial route and its two riverine side streets as the site of an important Middle Saxon settlement is thus untested but, while it seems clear that Norwich was no Ipswich or Hamwic (Southampton) at this period, the archaeological evidence, such as it is, probably points to a gradually developing urban community.

The economic base of such a community is unclear but there are hints of trade. The 1985 Fishergate site recovered a *sceat* or penny from Mercia and pottery sherds from the Rhineland. Similar pottery was located at Barn Road thirty years earlier. It is interesting that the Rose Lane pottery finds were made next to the site of the church of St Vedast (or SS Vaast and

Amand, two Flemish saints). This church is almost certainly of later, if still pre-Conquest, origin but the dedication to St Amand of Maastricht, a sixth-century Flemish saint, may be indicative of earlier trade contact with the Low Countries.

There is insufficient evidence to suggest whether parts of the settlement, on either bank of the river, were planned or merely grew up organically and the remains of buildings have yet to be located. It is possible that some churches may date from this period (examples as disparate as St Martin-at-Palace, St Michael Coslany, St Etheldreda and St John de Sepulchre have all been suggested) but none can be proven to be Middle Saxon in origin.

The apparent situation of either several small, distinct settlements or ribbon development on both banks of the river probably continued into the ninth century. It seems clear, however, that thereafter a developing social and economic impetus led to the transformation of settlement into a more dynamic whole by the early eleventh century at the latest, and probably by the tenth century. It is not known where this impetus found its genesis but the incursion of the Danes into East Anglia during the third quarter of the ninth century seems a likely source.

The Anglo-Scandinavian borough

The Danes effectively conquered East Anglia after the defeat and murder of the East Anglian king, Edmund, in 870. While a decade of fighting across southern England was to follow, culminating in Danish defeat at the Battle of Edington against Alfred in 878 and the Treaty of Wedmore, it is subsequently recorded in the *Anglo-Saxon Chronicle* that, in 880, the Danish host 'went from Cirencester into East Anglia, and occupied that land, and shared it out'. Occupation must, in large part, have taken the form of rural settlement, but the Danes also congregated in towns, as is known in the East Midlands with the Five Danish Boroughs of Nottingham, Derby, Lincoln, Leicester and Stamford. No mention is made of towns in Norfolk at this period, except that the Danish host wintered in Thetford in 870. It seems probable from a variety of evidence, however, that Norwich was becoming important as an urban centre.

Norwich retains a rich and importance inheritance which clearly dates from Danish occupation of the site. The most obvious evidence of this is that of street names with Danish formations (such as Fisher*gate* and Potter*gate* – the streets of the fishermen and potters) which were common in medieval Norwich. Many of these are known to have been coined as late as the fourteenth century (Westlegate) but they clearly reflect a considerable Anglo-Scandinavian heritage.

Most such names are related to streets. Indeed, it is interesting that few early topographical names can be shown to be Danish in origin. The significance of those that are is, however, great. The royal, and subsequently episcopal, manor of Thorpe to the east of the city is a Danish formation ('new settlement') while the area of Cow*holme* (ultimately part of the Cathedral Close) means 'water meadow' or 'flat ground' from the old Danish word 'holm'. The importance of Thorpe, which included land west of the river Wensum (such as Cowholme) as well as east, to the development of Norwich was to be considerable.

Church dedications also suggest Danish influence. The Viking Saint Olaf (or Olave) was not martyred until 1030 but there were nevertheless two churches dedicated to him in Norwich, emphasizing the residual importance of the Danish community in the eleventh century. In addition, it seems probable that the church of St Clement Colegate was a Danish foundation. St Clement is a most interesting parish. The extant building is predominantly a late medieval structure but the extent of the parish was once great, occupying large areas of the city both within and beyond the walls and possibly part of the early manor of Tokethorpe (from the Scandinavian personal name 'Toki' and 'thorpe'). Analysis of the medieval tithe pattern indicates that a number of the other parishes on the north bank of the river Wensum were created by being carved out of St Clement's parish, two-thirds of their tithes being passed on to the mother church.

12 *Map showing the probable line of the Anglo-Scandinavian or Anglo-Saxon defences and the location of probable pre-Conquest churches on the north bank of the river* (Jayne Bown).

Such a history does not, of course, make it Danish in origin, but only some fifty or so pre-Reformation dedications to St Clement are known and a number of these are located in notable Anglo-Scandinavian towns – Ipswich, Cambridge, Bedford and London are examples. St Clement was a popular saint in the Scandinavian lands – the Cathedral at Aarhus is dedicated to him – and was the patron saint of sailors, frequently being depicted with his anchor. A characteristic location of churches to St Clement in towns is near the river, often

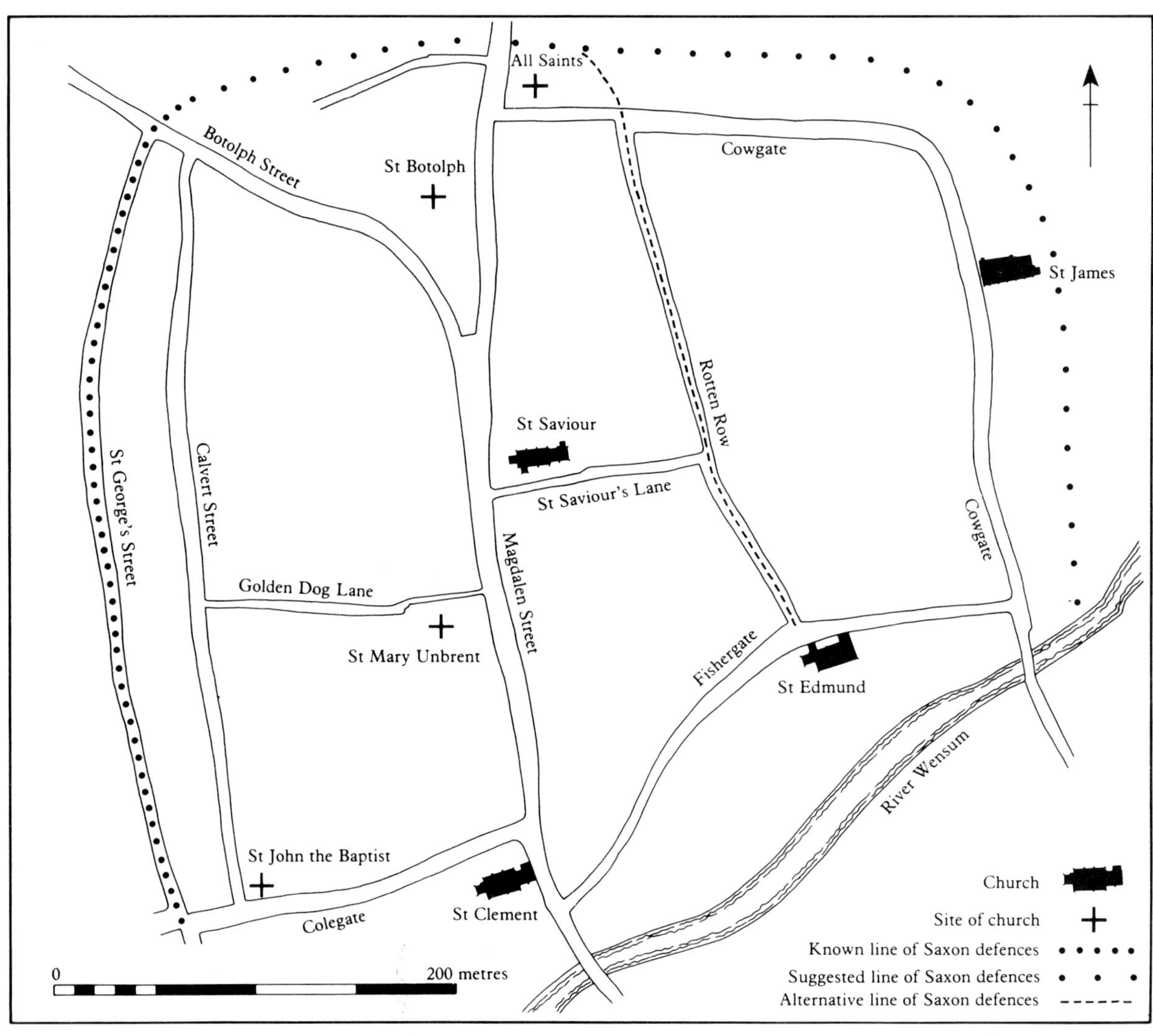

at the main river crossing, as in Bedford or Cambridge and in Norwich (at Fye Bridge, first recorded in the twelfth century but almost certainly in existence in the pre-Conquest period).

The location of St Clement, in the heart of the area probably known as Northwic and close to the only significant excavation of early material (that on Fishergate in 1985, where recovered artefacts included a linen smoother of 'Viking' date), suggests that the centre of Anglo-Scandinavian activity in Norwich was on the north bank of the river Wensum, the Danes co-occupying that part of the growing city which was apparently most densely occupied by the Anglo-Saxons. Archaeological evidence remains thin but there is some support for this assertion in the known location of a defensive ditch and bank which encircled this area, probably from the early tenth century.

The existence of such a defensive system was first suggested by topographical analysis of the street pattern of Norwich north of the river (**12**). This revealed interesting features. The alignment of St George's Street (historically Gildengate) runs northward from the river until it meets Botolph Street (largely lost after 1974). This alignment is paralleled by Calvert Street (Snaylgate) immediately to the east, both streets being continued in curving property boundaries north of Botolph Street to effect a junction with the principal north to south route of Magdalen Street (Fyebridgegate). East of Magdalen Street, the line of Cowgate runs eastward until it curves south to the river.

The effect of these alignments is to suggest a 'D'-shaped enclosure on the north bank of the river. Excavation in the 1970s and again in 1989–90 on either side of St George's Street (**13**) revealed a ditch with the remains of a defensive bank on its eastern side. This ditch had been recut twice and was infilled in the twelfth century. Dating of its construction is difficult (a radiocarbon date for one excavation suggests only some time in the tenth century)

13 *View of the Calvert Street excavations showing the Anglo-Scandinavian or Anglo-Saxon defensive ditch in the foreground (* Lee Martin*).*

but comparison with other enclosures would imply strongly that the earthwork is an Anglo-Scandinavian enclosure. Such defensive earthworks are known from Ipswich (where recent excavations suggest a construction of *c.* 912), Repton, Bedford and, most famously, Hedeby or Haithabu, the great Danish emporium on the Baltic.

The extent of the enclosure east of Magdalen Street has yet to be confirmed by excavation. Work in 1992 on the north to south part of Cowgate (now Whitefriars) has demonstrated that the street here is a post-Conquest creation, with deposits previously thought to be ditch fills being, most probably, infilling of lowlying land next to the river. It currently seems likely that any return to the river of a defensive alignment would be along Peacock Street (for-

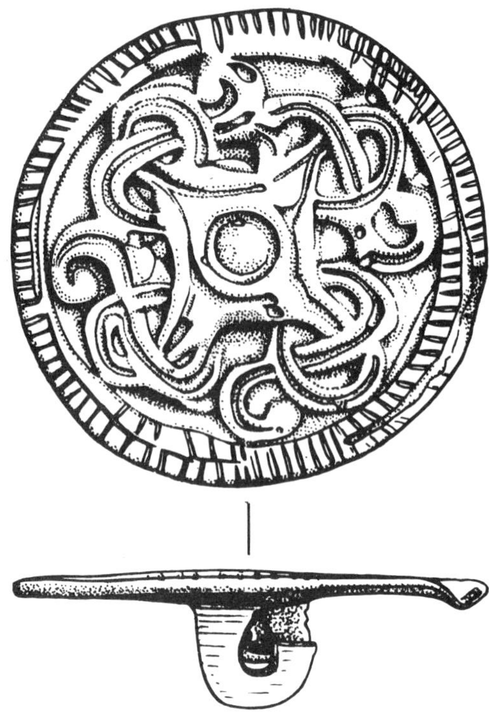

14 *Borre-style brooch recovered from the Anglia Television excavation in 1979 (*Ryszard Hajdul*).*

merly Rattenrowe). This would take advantage of natural protection from the course of the Dalymond stream which flowed to the river here and would make sense of early references to the edge of the borough. The western side of the defended enclosure would have been protected by the Muspole, an area of lowlying marshy ground. Again, such topographical positioning between protective streams or low-lying ground parallels other Anglo-Scandin-avian enclosures such as Bedford and Lincoln where streams mark the flanks of defended areas.

The defences would have been pierced by two streets, Botolph Street and Magdalen Street, requiring gates. Topographical analysis can suggest the location of these as well. Botolph Street is named after St Botolph's church (which disappeared in the sixteenth century), a dedication frequently given to churches close to gateways in urban defences (such as the

15 *Cross shaft with Scandinavian interlace recovered from a house demolished on Rose Lane in 1896 (*Karen Guffogg*).*

churches of St Botolph Aldersgate, Aldgate, Billingsgate and Bishopsgate in London, St Botolph Cambridge or St Botolph Colchester). St Botolph Norwich was not close to the later medieval city wall but was adjacent to the smaller, earlier, defended enclosure. Similarly, the position of a gateway at Magdalen Street is marked by the location of the church of All Saints (also lost in the sixteenth century). Here the church was so close that it can be suggested that it was originally part of the gate structure, as is known from examples at Canterbury.

While the extent of Anglo-Scandinavian Norwich is therefore not known from documentation, it is possible to imply a growing settlement from other evidence. This settlement was clearly no Jorvik, or even a Stamford or Derby, but was probably beginning to thrive. The greatest concentration of activity was almost certainly in the vicinity of St Clement's, although a further church dedicated to St Clement at the southern end of King Street may imply a small riverside settlement downstream (this was also the location of one of the two churches subsequently dedicated to St Olaf).

The greatest indication of Danish influence remains the legacy of Scandinavian nomenclature and artefacts. A late ninth-century sword was recovered from the river Wensum about 1854; tenth-century Borre-style brooches (**14**) have been discovered south of the river near Rose Avenue; a cross fragment (**15**) of tenth-century interlace was recovered from the site of the church of St Vedast on Rose Lane while, as late as the beginning of the twelfth century, an early capital for the cathedral was decorated with an intricate Urnes-style interlace.

Perhaps, however, the greatest contribution

16 *Coin of Aethelstan (924–39) minted in Norwich, the earliest reference to the settlement's name (*Norfolk Museums Service*).*

of the Danes was to define Norwich as a burh or borough; this is not clear from documentation but can be inferred from later activity. East Anglia fell to the Saxon king Edward the Elder in 917, Norwich thus returning to the English orbit. By the reign of Edward's son, Aethelstan (924–39), there is, at last, a positive indication of the settlement's growing status; among mint signatures of Aethelstan's coinage appears, for the first time, that of *Norvic* or Norwich (**16**).

2

The Late Saxon town

The establishment of a mint at Norwich in the second quarter of the tenth century implies that the settlement was a borough and that it was furnished, in part at least, with fortifications. Aethelstan's decrees of Grateley in *c*. 935 make it clear that mints should be within defended areas and located in towns. As the only known pre-Conquest defences in Norwich are those located on the north bank of the river Wensum, it seems reasonable to suppose that the mint was located here.

The settlement may have been gaining recognition as a growing town of importance but this is still not reflected in extant documentary sources. No mention of Norwich is made until the 980s when the *Liber Eliensis* or Book of Ely records that Abbot Brithnoth of Ely, when buying land in Cambridge, was assured by all there 'that Cambridge and Norwich and Ipswich and Thetford were of such liberty and dignity that if anyone bought land there he did not need witnesses'. This implies a well-established town and suggests that the settlement had been growing in status for the previous fifty years. The material evidence is, however, difficult to locate.

Most of the archaeological work of the last twenty-five years, and most work at any previous time, has been undertaken on the south bank of the river Wensum. This has frequently uncovered material of later Saxon date, but only rarely can this be demonstrated to be unequivocally of the tenth century. It is clear that there was tenth-century occupation but nothing apparently of the intensity to suggest the growing town implied by both mint status and the *Liber Eliensis* reference. It follows that the greatest concentration of people was elsewhere, almost certainly north of the river.

The north bank

Once again the absence of archaeological data from the north bank is a hindrance. The relative lack of recent development is complemented by the relative distance of the area from the Castle Museum. For much of the post-War period, casual finds uncovered by development were, and often still are, recorded by staff of the Castle Museum (usually during lunch hour). Distance clearly inhibits such casual recording and it has also been noted that, until the late 1970s, no member of staff lived to the north of the city and thus did not pass development sites on the way to and from work! In consequence, finds from this area were recorded infrequently.

The instigation of new procedures is now helping to establish a more systematic appraisal of building works throughout the city, but it will be some time before there is a more comprehensive dataset for the north bank area. The Fishergate excavation produced a corpus of pottery which suggests considerable tenth-century activity in the vicinity and the location of early churches and defences similarly implies occupation. Taken with the lack of evidence for the south bank it is thus probable that the town mentioned to Abbot Brithnoth when he visited Cambridge was largely clustered in an area either side of present-day Magdalen Street. It follows that opportunities for archaeological excavation need to be seized on the north bank in order to clarify the nature of the tenth-century borough and its economy.

The second documentary reference to Norwich is both more dramatic than the Abbot's excursion and forms the first such reference in the *Anglo-Saxon Chronicle*. It states that, in 1004, King Sweyn of Denmark 'came with his fleet to Norwich and completely burned and ravaged the borough'. As with so much of the early history of Norwich, the site of this disaster is unknown. It can be speculated again, however, that it was on the north bank, that part of the city known in later documentation as *in combusto* ('in the burnt area'). The city no doubt suffered numerous fires in the Middle Ages, and it would be too much to assert that *in combusto* refers to Sweyn's attack, but the possibility that it does must exist. It is interesting that, of all the many churches of the medieval city, only two had fire references in suffixes to their dedications: the churches of St Mary *Combuste* and St Margaret *in Combusto*. Both are now lost (St Mary amalgamated with St Saviour in the sixteenth century and St Margaret ultimately with St Paul) but both stood on Magdalen Street. St Margaret is late, probably founded about 1100, but St Mary may well have dated to the pre-Conquest period; it stood at the corner of Magdalen Street and Golden Dog Lane.

Sweyn's attack may have been devastating but it does not seem to have arrested the growth of Norwich. On the contrary, growth thereafter seems to have been little short of spectacular. Documentation remains very scanty (a reference to Canute at a battle near Norwich in 1014, but possibly referring to his activities with his father in 1004, and two wills are all that are known) but all other evidence suggests a burgeoning community. Norwich may have been 'completely burned and ravaged' in 1004

but, by 1066, it had at least twenty-five churches (and possibly as many as forty) with a population estimated between 5000 and 10,000 people.

The south bank

There is considerable topographical, ecclesiastical and archaeological evidence to support this concept of a rapidly developing borough. Most of it comes from the south bank of the river and, indeed, there does seem to have been an

17 *Walrus ivory pectoral cross found on Tombland in 1878 during construction of subterranean toilets; now in the Victoria and Albert Museum London (*Victoria and Albert Museum*).*

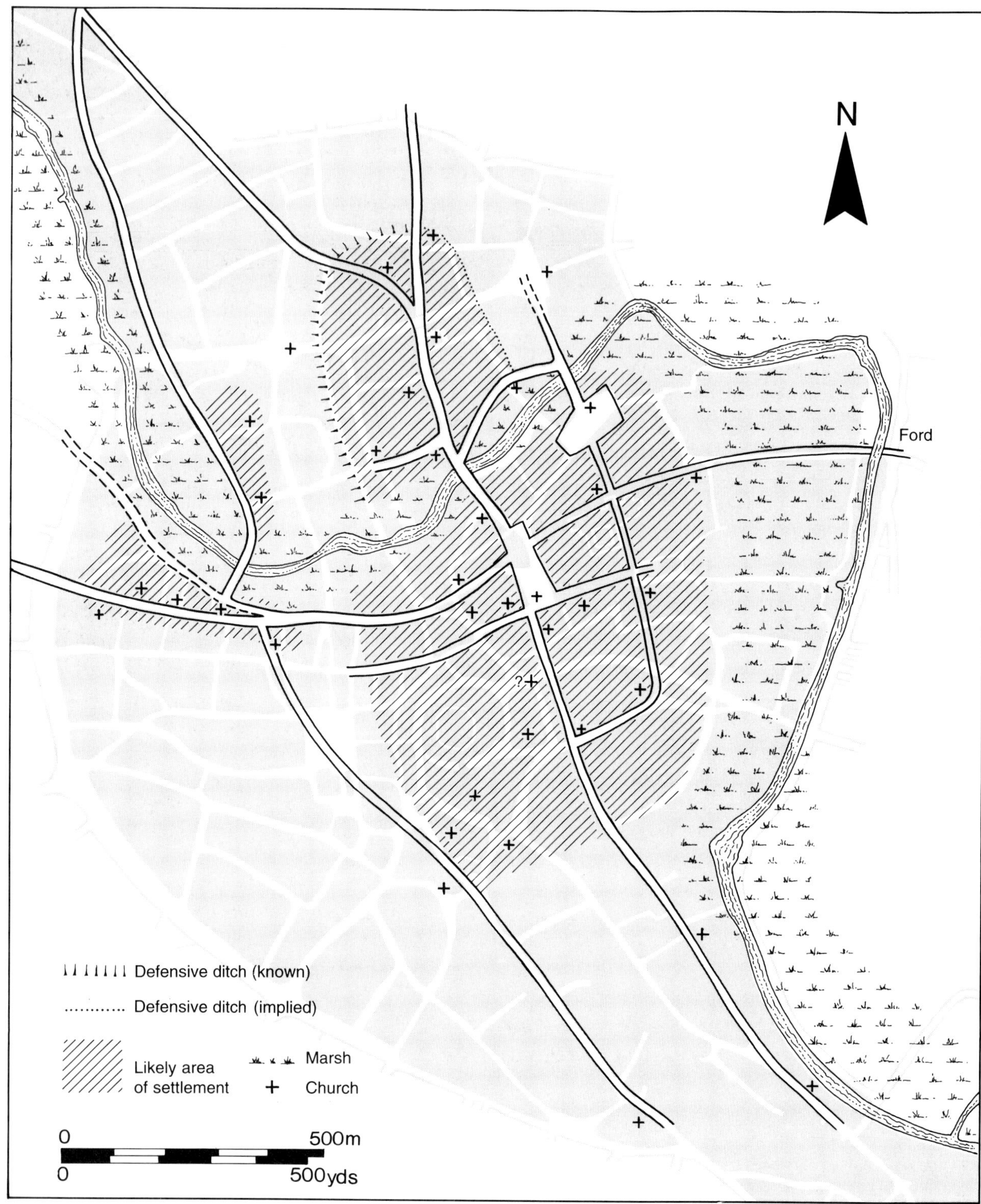

18 *Plan of the Late Saxon town showing a reconstructed street pattern and the sites of probable pre-Conquest churches* (Karen Guffogg).

extraordinary outbreak of development in this area. Analysis of this development is complicated by the imposition of the castle and cathedral precincts in the Norman period, but it is now becoming clear that the extent of occupation was very great, being bounded by the river to the north and east, running southward up the Ber Street escarpment and westward to the valley of the Great Cockey, a tributary of the Wensum.

The centre of this developing urban area was Tombland, the site of the market place with the place-name meaning 'empty' or 'open' space. It was a location which boasted a house belonging to the bishop at its northern end (where the Maid's Head Hotel now stands) and, reputedly, the 'palace' of the Earls of East Anglia to the south. The richest church in the borough, that of St Michael Tombland, was located here; the building was destroyed during the initial construction of the Cathedral Close in the 1090s, but the discovery of a walrus ivory pectoral cross during excavation of subterranean lavatories in 1878 (the finest piece of pre-Conquest art from the city) probably indicates its location (**17**).

Tombland itself survives and stands astride a relict pre-Conquest urban landscape. Streets to the north, south and, particularly, to the west can be suggested as Late Saxon in origin and it is possible to reconstruct the alignment of others within the area of the Cathedral Close (while a metalled road (**19**) predating the thirteenth-century Franciscan friary was uncovered to the south of the Close in 1993). Recent excavations imply that occupation spread as far as Timberhill to the south-west, across an area of some fifty hectares (125 acres), although the density of such occupation was probably patchy.

The reconstructed plan has considerable regularity and may possibly be the result of conscious town planning. Such an action would help to explain the rapid development of the borough in the first two-thirds of the eleventh century. A context could have been deliberate

19 *Metalled road excavated beneath the site of the Franciscan Friary, 1993 (*Phil Emery*).*

plantation by important magnates: the king, the earl, the bishop and the abbots of Bury and Ely are all known to have held land in Norwich before the Conquest.

The extent and shape of the town in the eleventh century is most eloquently expressed by its churches. Eight are recorded by name as existing before 1066 (All Saints, Christ Church, St Laurence, St Martin, St Mary, St Michael, SS Simon and Jude, and St Sepulchre). Others can be suggested by architectural detail, dedication or excavation. This last has discovered a previously unrecorded timber church demolished to make way for the castle, and located burials which suggest two, and possibly three, other lost and unrecorded Saxon churches.

The density of probable Late Saxon churches is particularly apparent in the vicinity of

Tombland, where many either stood or appear to have stood on street corners. Evidence can be cited of the churches of St Mary the Less, St Michael-at-Pleas, St Peter Hungate and SS Simon and Jude of extant examples and probably St Cuthbert, St Ethelbert, St Mary-in-the-Marsh, Christ Church, St Helen, St John the Evangelist and St Vedast of lost examples (the church dedicated to St Cuthbert, immediately south of the Saxon market place, is an unusual one in southern England and is paralleled by a similar example close to the

20 *The east wall of the church of St Martin-at-Palace showing Anglo-Saxon long-and-short work in Barnack limestone (*Kirk Laws-Chapman*).*

market in Thetford). This consistent positioning, with the two rich churches of St Michael Tombland and St Martin-at-Palace (**20**) occupying central sites within open areas (Tombland and *Bichil* respectively), enhances the possibility of deliberate planning.

As mentioned in Chapter 1 (pp. 24–5), the church of St Vedast was originally dedicated to two Flemish saints, Vaast and Amand (Vedast was subsequently anglicized to St Faith). The church was demolished in the sixteenth century but its site may indicate the location of a small, pre-Conquest, Flemish community. This would emphasize the growing commercial importance of Norwich, a borough now of considerable administrative significance for both secular and ecclesiastical powers and with an increasingly diverse economic base. The town was becoming a major market centre, trading in goods to its hinterland, the region and across the North Sea.

International trade was probably quite restricted although archaeological evidence has demonstrated eleventh-century contacts with Scandinavia, the Low Countries and the Rhineland. Regional and local trade was clearly much more important. The population of East Anglia, and particularly of eastern Norfolk, was remarkably dense by 1066 compared with much of the rest of lowland England. Unlike other southern shires, however, few towns had developed in Norfolk, so that Norwich already dominated a rich agricultural area. Its remarkable growth must have owed much to this fortunate circumstance.

The river was very much at the heart of the developing borough, serving a community which occupied both banks. The north bank was not deserted when spectacular growth became evident to the south. A decline to subordinate status must have set in, however, as was made only too obvious by the name given to the medieval leet or administrative area of the north bank – *ultra aquam* or 'over the water', presumably away from what was now the centre of the settlement or the centres

21 *Eleventh-century wickerwork fence used to consolidate the foreshore. St Martin-at-Palace Plain 1981 (*Brian Ayers*).*

of administrative control (the post-Conquest castle, cathedral and market place/tollhouse). River trade, however, probably maintained activity on Colegate and Fishergate.

Such trade certainly helped to develop areas to the south at places like St Martin-at-Palace Plain. Here, a gravel terrace at the northern edge of *Bichil* (bitch's hill or beak-like hill, first recorded at the end of the twelfth century), was consolidated by the dumping of animal dung, rubbish and straw, held in place by small wickerwork fences (**21**). The resulting surface or 'hard' next to the river would have been used to beach river craft, and probably the occasional seagoing vessel, for the loading and unloading of goods over the side. Excavation uncovered evidence for such surfaces upstream of Whitefriars Bridge in 1979 and downstream

in 1981. The second, and larger, excavation also located evidence for boat-building in the form of timbers set into the gravel foreshore which probably formed the basis of frameworks for construction in a manner paralleled by discoveries in Schleswig, northern Germany.

Buildings

The gravel terrace upon which the dumped surfaces were constructed sloped uphill to the south and timber buildings were erected upon the slope, next to the street frontage. Two types were identified, the one built above discrete post-holes and the other above post-in-slot footings. The larger buildings appear to have stood at right angles to the street with smaller structures parallel to the street at the rear (precision is difficult because complete ground plans could not be recovered due to destruction of the evidence by the construction of later buildings).

Infilling of the walls was probably effected with wattle-and-daub (some was found in one of the post-holes) and roofs could have been thatched. These timber structures may have been houses for domestic occupation but it is just as likely that they formed a type of warehouse or store as no evidence was found of domestic rubbish disposal. It is possible to visualize a small commercial community working next to the river, especially as fragments of similar structures were observed immediately downstream during excavations in 1972.

The problem of damage to archaeological deposits by development in later centuries is common to all towns where density of occupation has gradually increased. The survival of evidence for pre-Conquest buildings in Norwich as elsewhere is particularly rare as secular buildings, and probably most ecclesiastical ones, were built of wood. Very little of the historic core of the city contains waterlogged deposits, which enhance the preservation of the wooden elements of buildings, and thus the archaeological clues to such buildings consist of fragile features such as infilled post-holes.

22 *Excavated remains of an eleventh-century sunken-featured building off Rose Lane, 1993 (Phil Emery).*

Dense development over most of the last thousand years has ensured that much destruction of these features has taken place, leaving only tantalizing fragments of building plans to suggest location, size and orientation.

These fragments have been seen on numerous excavations in the city, on both banks of the river (a notable example being located beneath the bank of the later medieval defences at Barn Road in 1954–55). The first complete ground plans of secular buildings, however, have now been recovered. Excavations on the 2.4 hectare (6 acre) Castle Mall site between 1989 and 1991 uncovered two such structures in late 1990. These were of a third type of building, one which incorporated either cellars or, more probably, sunken floors, supplementing discrete post-hole and post-in-slot examples. Two further examples were excavated between King Street and Rose Lane in 1992 (**22**).

The sunken floor in each was created by the excavation of a large straight-sided pit, subrectangular or square in the case of the four Norwich structures, perhaps to a depth of 1–2m (the full depth had been truncated at Castle Mall by eighteenth- and nineteenth-century landscaping and, in the case of the buildings near King Street and Rose Lane, by thirteenth-

century and later works for the Franciscan friary). Vertical posts were then set out at intervals around the base of the pit with horizontal planks behind the posts, between them and the pit sides. The posts and planks thus revetted the sides and created a small, subterranean room. The tops of the posts were probably jointed into a sill beam with the superstructure of the building rising out of the upper face of the beam, the implication being that these were simple timber-framed structures (**23**). The building near King Street was furnished with a hearth of reused Roman bricks and it and the Rose Lane structure had ledges which may have served as bases for wooden benches.

Examples of such 'sunken-featured' buildings are known from other pre-Conquest urban sites such as Ipswich and, more famously, York. Future work in Norwich ought to be able to identify the relationship of these and other buildings to tenemental organization. The Castle Mall work has revealed shallow linear ditches which may represent property boundaries, and at least one boundary could be suggested from excavation at St Martin-at-Palace Plain in 1981. It has not yet been possible, however, to argue convincingly for the survival of pre-Conquest property boundaries, through known medieval tenement patterns, to the complex post-medieval tenemental organization which is now largely disappearing or has indeed disappeared.

Churches

It is possible to establish early churchyard boundaries, as has been done recently on the north side of the church of St John Timberhill. Here, a curving ditch was shown to mark the edge of the early graveyard (although it may have been cut in the post-Conquest period). The graveyard bounded by the ditch went out of use in the fifteenth century (the church itself remains in use to this day) but the curve of the boundary was marked by buildings off an alleyway (Grout's Thoroughfare) until at least 1883.

23 *Reconstruction of two eleventh-century buildings excavated at Castle Mall, 1990 (*Karen Guffogg*).*

St John's church probably contains Late Saxon fabric, as does the church of St Martin-at-Palace. Here, the east wall of the chancel has long-and-short work, datable to the Conquest period (see **20**), and excavation has revealed characteristic Saxo-Norman flint, chalk and gravel foundations. The building was preceded by two earlier timber structures, one of these probably being furnished with at least some well-appointed graves. Fragments of a limestone grave cover with interlace decoration, rare in East Anglia, were uncovered by the excavation. Some pre-Conquest church foundations, however, have disappeared altogether.

One such was a church of unknown dedication which stood where offices for Anglia Television now stand. Excavation ahead of construction of these offices in 1979 uncovered the complete ground plan of a post-in-slot timber church with a rectangular nave and a square chancel (**24**). The building was furnished with a font (the soakaway for which was located) and possibly with a belfry (supported on a post set centrally within the nave). Graves were located around the building although not within it, consistent with Anglo-Saxon burial practice. The building was deliberately destroyed after the Norman Conquest, almost certainly to allow the construction of the north-east bailey of the castle.

The church seems to have existed for only some seventy-five years. The graveyard was thus of particular importance because it contained individuals who were almost exclusively Anglo-Saxon or Anglo-Scandinavian without the possibility of mixing with burials of later date. Analysis of the skeletons, therefore, enabled a study of an essentially pre-Conquest population. The assemblage was small (only about 130 individuals, as not all the graveyard was dug) but it showed that the people in

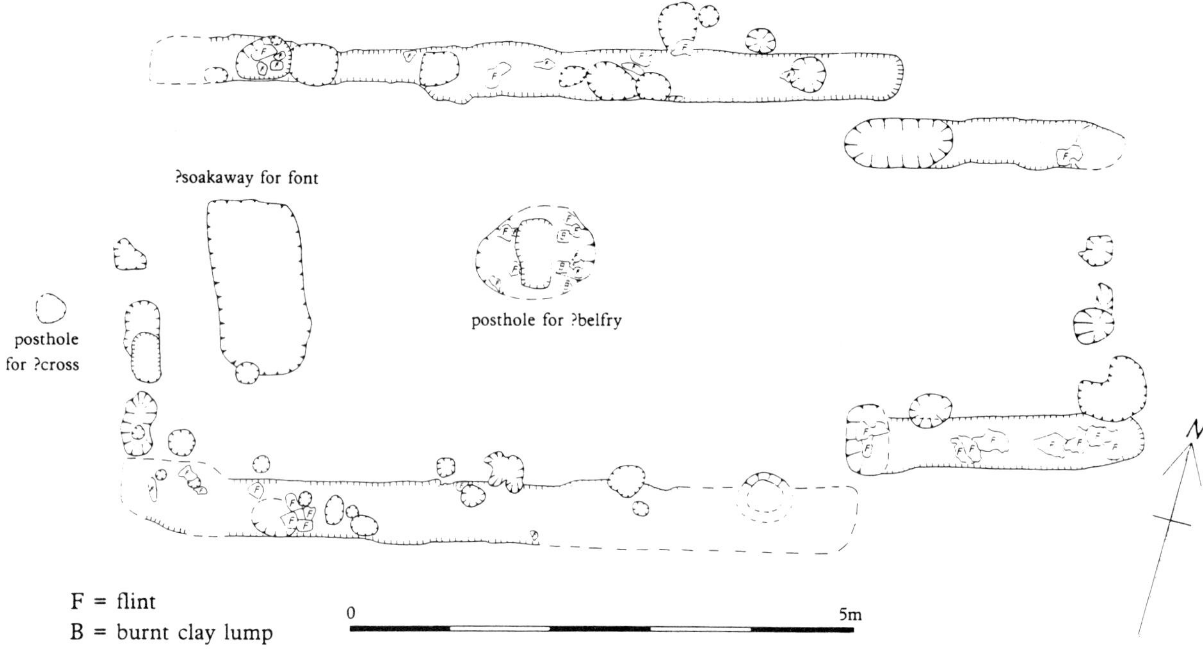

24 *Plan of the eleventh-century timber church destroyed by clearance for the north-east bailey of the castle. Anglia Television site 1979* (Philip Williams).

25 *Skull of individual from the 1979 Anglia Television site showing pronounced sutures indicative of rickets* (David Wicks).

this parish at least were poor and generally malnourished. Rickets was common among the child burials and the adults showed signs of having suffered similarly in youth (**25**). The skeletons of the adult males were particularly notable for the muscle strains evident in the bone, implying lives full of hard, physical labour.

Trade and industry

Much of this labour probably went into the task of everyday existence in a society where great effort would be required to provide food, shelter and warmth. It is possible that the tasks of some of these men also included industrial work such as quarrying. By the Middle Ages, the exploitation of quarries in and around Norwich was very great and it is likely that the tradition began in the pre-Conquest period, providing flint and lime mortar for the few stone churches as well as lime to spread on the town fields.

The quarrying trade can only be surmised (although there is increasing archaeological evidence for the extraction of iron ore from the river gravels) but another pre-Conquest industry which would have entailed consider-

26 *Excavated Thetford-type ware pottery kiln, Bedford Street 1980. The firing chamber is in the foreground, the 'combustion' chamber where the pots were fired is behind it with two pedestals around which the pots were stacked. Remnant magnetic dating techniques suggest a central date for the last firing of* c. AD*1000 (Brian Ayers).*

27 *Cut-away reconstruction of Thetford-type ware pottery kiln; the dome was probably constructed of turf and dismantled after each firing (*Susan G. White, Norfolk Landscape Archaeology*).*

able labour was that of potting. Evidence for this is now extensive. Kilns seem to have operated along both sides of Bedford Street and Lobster Lane (historically Pottergate, 'the street of the potters') producing an earthenware pottery known as Thetford-type ware (large quantities of waster vessel fragments have been recorded in watching briefs and excavations over the last twenty-five years) (**26**). Suitable clay existed in the Norwich area but not that close to Pottergate, and it must have been imported.

The pottery industry produced a range of vessel types although the most common was the jar, followed by small lamps. The vessels were unglazed but occasionally decorated with rouletting or, in the case of spouted pitchers and large storage jars, with applied strips of clay thumbed to make a pattern. The kilns were pits cut into the ground, one of which was excavated in 1980. It was oval in shape with a stoke-pit and two pedestals within the main combustion chamber. Pots were stacked around these pedestals and the full kiln was probably roofed with turf (**27**).

Pottery produced in such kilns was distributed over a wide area, not just in Norwich, where it occurs on all eleventh-century pre-Conquest sites, but also to much of the rest of East Anglia and other parts of eastern England. It may even have been traded across the North Sea; Thetford-type pottery found on the Bryggen excavations at Bergen in Norway may have been manufactured in Norwich (although there were also production centres in Ipswich and Thetford itself). Earlier commentators frequently confused the fabric with Roman material, leading to erroneous conclusions. The ware continued to be made in Norwich into the twelfth century.

Other craft industries existed within the growing borough. The strong Anglo-Scandinavian inheritance is seen in Borre-style brooches (see **14**), only three of which have been found in Norwich, all within 50 metres (165ft) of each other near Rose Avenue, implying a workshop in the locality. Other metalwork was probably manufactured in the city, possibly including an eleventh-century Ringerike-style mount from the Magistrates' Court site, which may have formed part of a saddle.

The saddle itself, of course, would have been made of leather and evidence for leather working has also been found, particularly on riverside sites. Here shoemakers' and cobblers' waste indicate that the animals which were being brought into the borough were not slaughtered solely for their meat. Tanners must have existed to supply the leatherworkers and the finished items of shoes, clothing and utensils would have been sold back to the countryside as well as to the inhabitants of the borough. Combs of antler and horn were manufactured in the town, comb-making waste being found on Fishergate in 1985.

Other industries can be recognized on the river margins. The retting of flax seems to have taken place at St Martin-at-Palace Plain, where stakes driven into the gravel foreshore may have been used to tether the flax (flax seeds were recovered in soil samples taken during

28 *Bronze strap-end with a naked figure; Anglia Television site 1979 (Ryszard Hajdul).*

excavation in 1979). Woodworking can be observed in excavated archaeological material, such as the remains of an oak box with dove-tailed or rabbetted joints or an ash core from the turning of a wooden bowl. Analysis of timbers recovered from the waterfront suggests that coppicing was practised.

Eleventh-century Norwich is thus gradually becoming more visible, mainly through the medium of archaeological excavation. It is possible that the churches of St Martin-at-Palace and St John Timberhill contain work of Late Saxon date and it has been argued that architectural work of similar date can be seen in churches such as St Gregory. Analysis of later tithe patterns suggests that St Gregory may have been an early parish which was subdivided following the creation of the parishes of St Laurence, St Margaret Westwick, St Swithin and St Benedict, probably all in the first half of the eleventh century. Largely, however, the pre-Conquest borough survives only in the inherited topography and below-ground archaeology. These nevertheless contain sufficient information to suggest a vibrant and rapidly-growing town with a diverse economic base and an increasingly complex social organization.

The borough of Norwich was Anglo-Scandinavian as much as it was Anglo-Saxon, with a Nordic tradition probably best exemplified by the pre-1066 obligation on the citizens to provide the king with a bear. This information lies within the Norman Domesday Book, a post-Conquest document which allows a glimpse of Norwich at the time of the Battle of Hastings. The glimpse thus afforded complements the evidence of the topography and archaeology, providing a framework for the late pre-Conquest discoveries and a background for the great changes which the Norman Conquest brought to the settlement. Anglo-Saxon Norwich had come to dominate its local area by the mid-eleventh century; the Normans would extend this local importance to regional supremacy.

3

Norman Norwich –
the secular town

The Norman impact upon Norwich was extraordinary, even by the standards of that extraordinarily energetic people. Within a generation following 1066, the basic urban topography had been changed more utterly than would be effected by any subsequent change prior to the twentieth century. The Normans seem to have found a thriving and growing borough, but they stamped their authority upon the settlement with such thoroughness that the modern geography of the historic core is fundamentally an Anglo-Norman and not just an Anglo-Saxon construct.

The Normans influenced every sphere of life. It is generally true that, at a base cultural level, it remains difficult (if not impossible) to differentiate Saxon occupation of the mid-eleventh century from that of the early Norman period, as underlined by the discovery at Castle Mall in 1989 of a bowl in a fabric usually dated to about 1100 but with stamped decoration of apparently earlier date. The establishment of major institutions such as the castle and the cathedral, however, ensured a domination of the borough by the new regime. Norman influence was indeed so pervasive between 1066 and the end of the twelfth century that it is easier to discuss the development of Norwich at this time in two parts: secular and ecclesiastical.

The single most important source for an initial understanding of Norwich in the years immediately after the Battle of Hastings is that provided by the Normans themselves – the entry concerning Norwich in the Domesday Book of 1086. Norwich is fortunate in that its entry is in Little Domesday, the volume covering eastern England which seems to be an earlier stage in the compilation process that went to produce the Great Domesday. Entries in the latter seem to be edited versions of more detailed data, data which therefore survives for Norwich. This both assists and complicates because, as always with historical research, the more data that is available, the more questions can be asked.

Domesday Book paints a picture of a town fallen on hard times by 1086. A population comprising some 1320 burgesses in 1066 had fallen to one of 655 burgesses. It seems likely that the effects of the Conquest and its aftermath had reduced the financial status of some of the burgesses to that of *bordar* or smallholder class (there were 480 of these in 1086 but none were mentioned for 1066), while 22 burgesses had quit the borough and fled to Beccles in Suffolk. The document complains that 'those fleeing and the others remaining have been utterly devastated partly because of Earl R(alph)'s forfeitures [Ralph was Earl of Norfolk and Suffolk until 1075, when he rebelled unsuccessfully against the Crown], partly because of fires, partly because of the King's tax, partly by Waleran [who held the borough in fee and farmed the tax]'.

This makes gloomy reading (and possibly represents a compilation by a surviving member

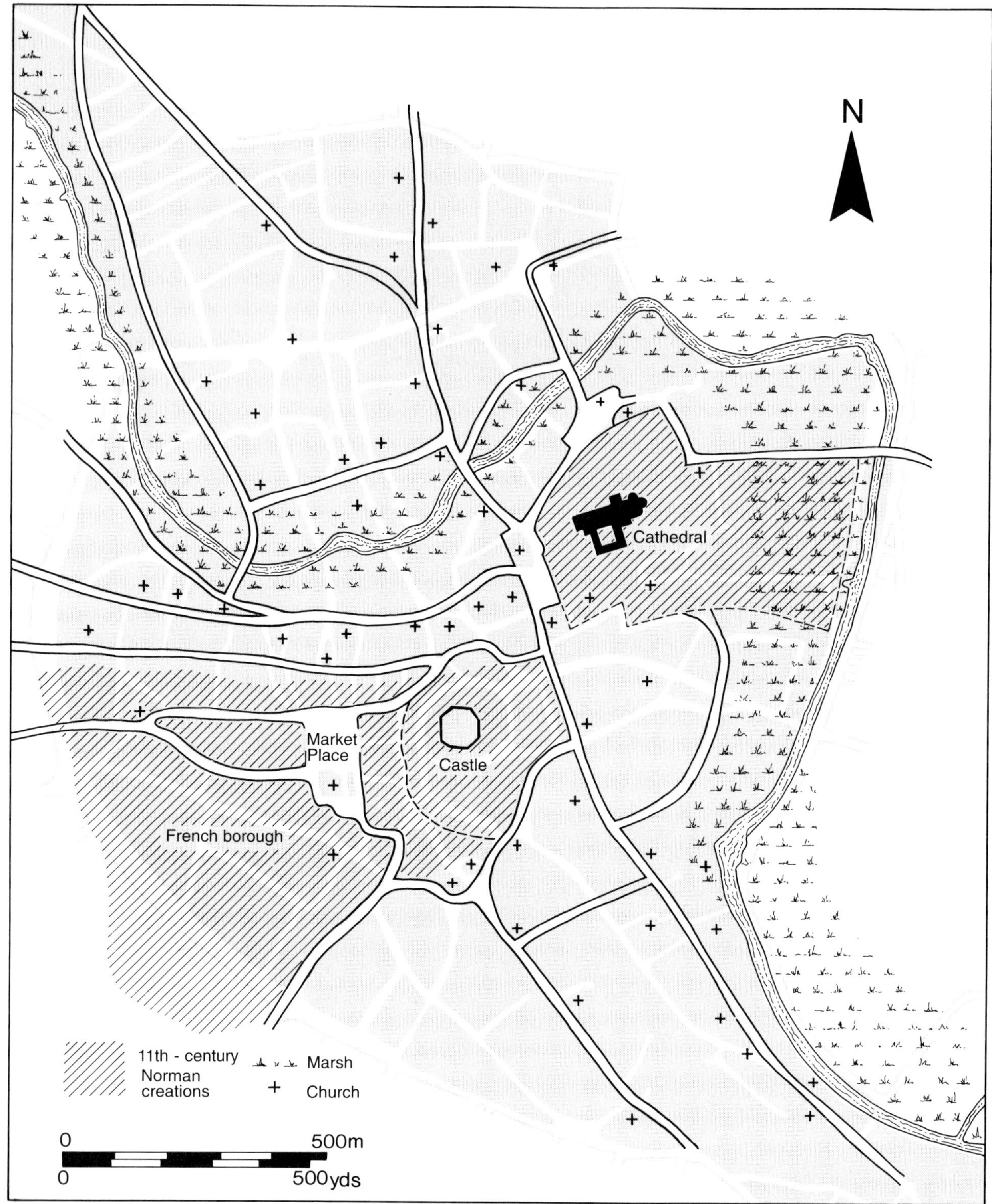

29 *Map of the Norman town showing the extent of the Castle precinct, the 'French Borough', the Cathedral Close, the locations of churches and Norman expansion to the south and north-east (*Karen Guffogg*).*

of the pre-Conquest administration) but it is also clear from the account that the infrastructure of the borough was already diverse. Between 25 and 40 churches seem to have been in existence by 1066 and at least one further foundation is recorded before 1075. A castle was defensible by 1075 and a new borough had been laid out to the west of the Anglo-Saxon town. Devastation in the years leading to 1086 had clearly been considerable (and would be followed by more disruption in the 1090s) but the establishment of institutions such as the castle would have a profound, and largely beneficial, impact upon the settlement's fortunes.

Norwich Castle

The castle, a royal rather than a baronial foundation, was probably under construction before the end of the 1060s as an earthwork and timber fortification. The provision of necessary space entailed the demolition of at least 98 houses which were now *'in occupatione castelli'* ('occupied by the castle') according to Domesday Book. This clearance may have involved the demolition of at least two churches as well. One of these, excavated in 1979, was mentioned above (p. 37); the other lay beneath the rampart of the south bailey and was excavated in 1989.

Work on the castle was sufficiently far advanced by 1075 for the fortress to withstand a siege when the Constable, Ralph de Guader, rebelled against the king (a hoard of William I pennies, discovered on London Street in 1972, may have been hidden at this time). The castle was invested by Lanfranc, Archbishop of Canterbury, who wrote an account to the Conqueror in Normandy when the garrison surrendered. This, probably the earliest English battle dispatch, read that:

> ...Norwich Castle is surrendered and the Britons [Bretons] who were in it and had lands in the English land, life being granted to them with limbs have sworn that within

forty days they will go from your Kingdom....In the same Castle have remained Bishop Geoffrey, W. de Warenna, Robert Malet and 300 men in armour with them, with Crossbowmen and many artificers of machines. All noise of wars (God pitying) is quiet in the English land....

The detail 'with limbs' was important for the besieged: rebellious Bretons at Winchester in the same year were maimed and blinded. The respite for the Bretons of Norwich was brief, however, as the unforgiving Conqueror punished them at Christmas 1075:

> Some of them were blinded,
> Some of them were banished,
> Some were brought to shame.
> So all traitors to the king
> Were laid low.

It would be too much to expect the recent (1989–91) large-scale excavations at Norwich Castle to reveal direct evidence for the siege. Indirectly, however, the evidence suggests that the 1075 castle may have only occupied that area now occupied by the great mound or motte with perhaps a small bailey. It seems likely that the great south bailey is a late eleventh-century creation, as is probably the north-east bailey.

Support for a hypothesis that the original castle may have consisted of a smaller motte with an associated ringwork of ditches, both of which were subsequently amalgamated to form the existing great mound, is found in interpretation of observations made in 1968 during construction of museum stores. The 1960s was such a dire decade for archaeology that even a museum building could be erected on an internationally important site without prior excavation, but surviving photographs seem to illustrate an early mound beneath the later stone keep.

Construction of the castle certainly continued after the 1075 rebellion and it probably grew to occupy 5.6 hectares (14 acres) by about

1100. Its position was at the northern end of the Ber Street hill, overlooking the river to the north and east. The extant mound is thus partly natural and partly artificial, the mound ditch separating it from the hill to the south. A partial section was excavated through the mound in 1906 for the construction of an extension to the Shirehall. This has recently been supplemented by a small excavation through part of the ditch fill below the castle bridge in 1990. These excavations demonstrate that the mound was both steeper and had a deeper ditch than appears today.

Although the castle may have started as a ringwork with a small motte, its final Norman form was that of a motte and bailey castle. In the case of Norwich there were two baileys,

30 *East exterior elevation of the keep of Norwich Castle by William Wilkins prior to nineteenth-century refacing. The arch below the (now destroyed) entrance tower leads into an early vault which survives (see fig. 53) (Norfolk Museums Service, Norwich Castle Museum).*

that to the north-east being known as Castle Meadow and almost certainly providing grazing for the herds and flocks of the garrison. Excavation has revealed parts of the ditches for both the south bailey and the north-east bailey, and the general disposition of the defences is now largely known. This is more remarkable than it sounds as landscaping in 1738, and again in 1862, had so thoroughly levelled the castle earthworks that the alignment of the ditches was lost and reconstructions as late as 1975, using all the available non-archaeological evidence, made considerable plotting errors.

The dearth of good building stone in Norfolk meant that the castle was always substantially an earthwork fortification. Stone monuments were constructed, however, most notably that of the keep. This extraordinary building survives, albeit much mutilated on the interior and refaced in an unfortunate manner on the exterior in 1834–9. The building accounts are

not known to exist and the structure is generally held to be attributable to the reign of Henry I (1100–35), largely on the grounds of stylistic comparison (notably with Falaise in Normandy) and masons' marks which are paralleled at the better documented cathedral. Recently it has been argued convincingly that the structure could date from as early as 1095. It is certainly a remarkable building with a wealth of detailing, both on the exterior façades (copied in the nineteenth-century refacing) and on interior motifs, which is almost unique for the period in England.

Stone for the facing of the keep was brought from Normandy and Northamptonshire, although the bulk of the fabric is constructed of local flint and lime mortar. Other stone monuments within the castle of twelfth-century date probably included the south gate (the site remains unexcavated) and possibly, at the foot of the mound bridge, a further gatehouse. This was replaced or enlarged in the early thirteenth century and massive remains of the flint and mortar structure of this later building, together with dressings of limestone, were uncovered in recent excavations (p. 72).

After the keep, however, the most spectacular surviving monument at the castle is the bridge to the mound. This structure, probably late twelfth- or early thirteenth-century in date, was refaced in the early nineteenth century, but excavations in 1990 and 1992 have demonstrated that it is substantially late Norman. It is formed of two abutments, the southern one of which has a buried plinth of eight courses of chamfered Caen stone beneath a faced wall also of Caen stone (**31**). Above, remains of a medieval gravel road surface survive beneath the modern tarmac.

The northern abutment has an infilled void, probably a counterweight pit for the drawbridge of another gatehouse which stood on the bridge until the eighteenth century. Linking the abutments are two arches of limestone, both substantially medieval with evidence of a removable timber roadway between them. The

timber was subsequently replaced, presumably by a vault, which was itself renewed in brick in 1830. The underside of the keystone is inscribed 'May 19 1830', a most helpful aid to the archaeologist!

The castle, being a royal foundation, was outside the jurisdiction of the borough. It occupied its own Liberty or Fee and the land of the Fee extended beyond the castle defences on all sides, most notably to the west. Here the ditch of the castle is now followed by a road (confusingly named Castle Meadow, 'borrowing' the place-name from the north-east bailey). West of this, however, is a street which runs concentrically with the ditch, now divided into London Street, Castle Street and Back of the Inns. This formed the boundary to the Fee, the boundary perhaps being marked by posts with plaques bearing the royal arms set upon them. Four such plaques were discovered in 1964, each pierced by several small nail holes (**32**). The Fee boundary itself may have been marked elsewhere by a ditch, as off Timberhill, where excavation in 1989 revealed such a feature.

The French Borough

The establishment of the castle was initially the responsibility of Earl Ralph. He also founded, with the king, a borough for their Norman-French compatriots. This borough, referred to in Domesday Book as for the 'Franci de Norwic', lay to the west of the castle on land which had probably served as open fields for the pre-Conquest Anglo-Scandinavian town. This much is implied by the name 'Mancroft' subsequently applied to the whole area. Mancroft means '(ge)maene croft' or 'common enclosure', 'common land', while the possibility has been suggested that part of the street alignment immediately west of the Market Place has a distinctive reverse 'S'-pattern typical of communities which have developed from earlier agricultural land. The church of St Peter Mancroft, by the later Middle Ages the most important church in the city, is probably the

ELEVATION OF BURIED
PART OF CASTLE BRIDGE

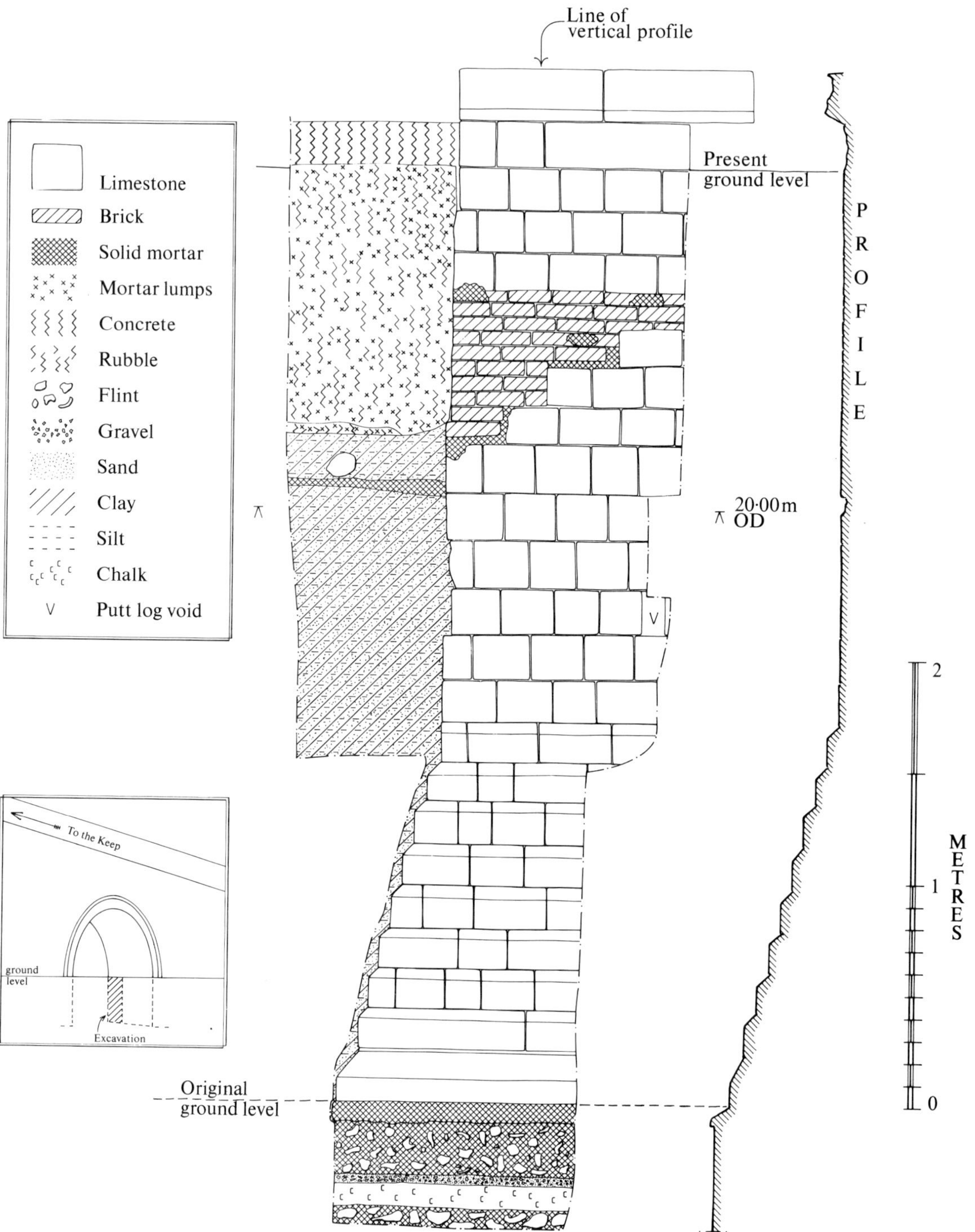

31 *Elevation and profile of the excavated base of the south abutment to the Castle Bridge showing the Caen stone facings and the plinth of nine chamfered risers, now beneath the Castle Gardens (* Hoste Spalding *).*

32 *Plaque (one of several) with the royal arms and nail holes found in 1964 and possibly mounted originally on posts to mark the edge of the royal liberty or 'Fee' of the castle (Bill Milligan).*

'certain church' which was also founded by Earl Ralph.

The French Borough was laid out around a large rectangular market place with two main streets leading westward, Upper Newport (now Bethel Street) and Lower Newport (St Giles Street). Two other churches, St Giles and St Stephen, were also founded. The borough was a remarkably rare creation, the only parallel being a similar borough at Nottingham. To date, there has been hardly any archaeological excavation within its area, although chance finds have been reported from a number of sites. These rarely predate the twelfth century, indicating that potential for understanding the development of the Norman town, unhindered by earlier Anglo-Saxon settlement, is considerable.

The Jewry

The eastern edge of the borough was probably marked by the line of the Great Cockey stream, the eastern bank of this stream being the boundary of the Castle Fee. Between the castle and the French Borough, and partly within the borough, was an area largely occupied as a Jewish Quarter (**33**). Predominantly grouped in and around Saddlegate (now White Lion Street) and the Haymarket, the Jews of Norwich formed one of the most important such communities in England.

There is no evidence that Jews lived in Norwich, or indeed England, before the Conquest. A community was established in Norwich by 1144 and may date from 1135, while a man called 'Isaac' is mentioned in Domesday Book. The concentration of Jews near the castle (although not all lived here) must have been for royal protection and is paralleled in other towns.

The Jewish community in Norwich is comparatively well documented. Archaeologically, however, there is as yet little evidence for it. Material recovered on the site of Littlewoods store (between the Market and the Castle Fee) in 1962 included a stone column with characteristic Norman tooling which may have come from the synagogue known to have stood hereabouts, which was either burnt down in 1286 or demolished in 1290. A bronze bowl, now in Oxford (the 'Bodleian Bowl'), was discovered in Norfolk in or before 1696. It is inscribed with a rabbinical inscription and is thought to have originated with the Norwich community. The greatest surviving Jewish artefact, however, is Jurnet's house on King Street.

Jurnet's Hall or the Music House is a three-storey building which stands on the east side of King Street next to the river Wensum (about 500m (1650ft) south-east of the main area of Jewish settlement). At right-angles to the street frontage, it is built of flint with a vault of freestone on the ground floor and may have been augmented with a further range to the south. Ground-floor window openings survive, as do part of a stair and column shafts for a doorway. A mason's mark, identical to those on the infirmary at the cathedral, would suggest a construction date of about 1175, making the building the oldest surviving house in the city. It was probably built for Jurnet, a wealthy

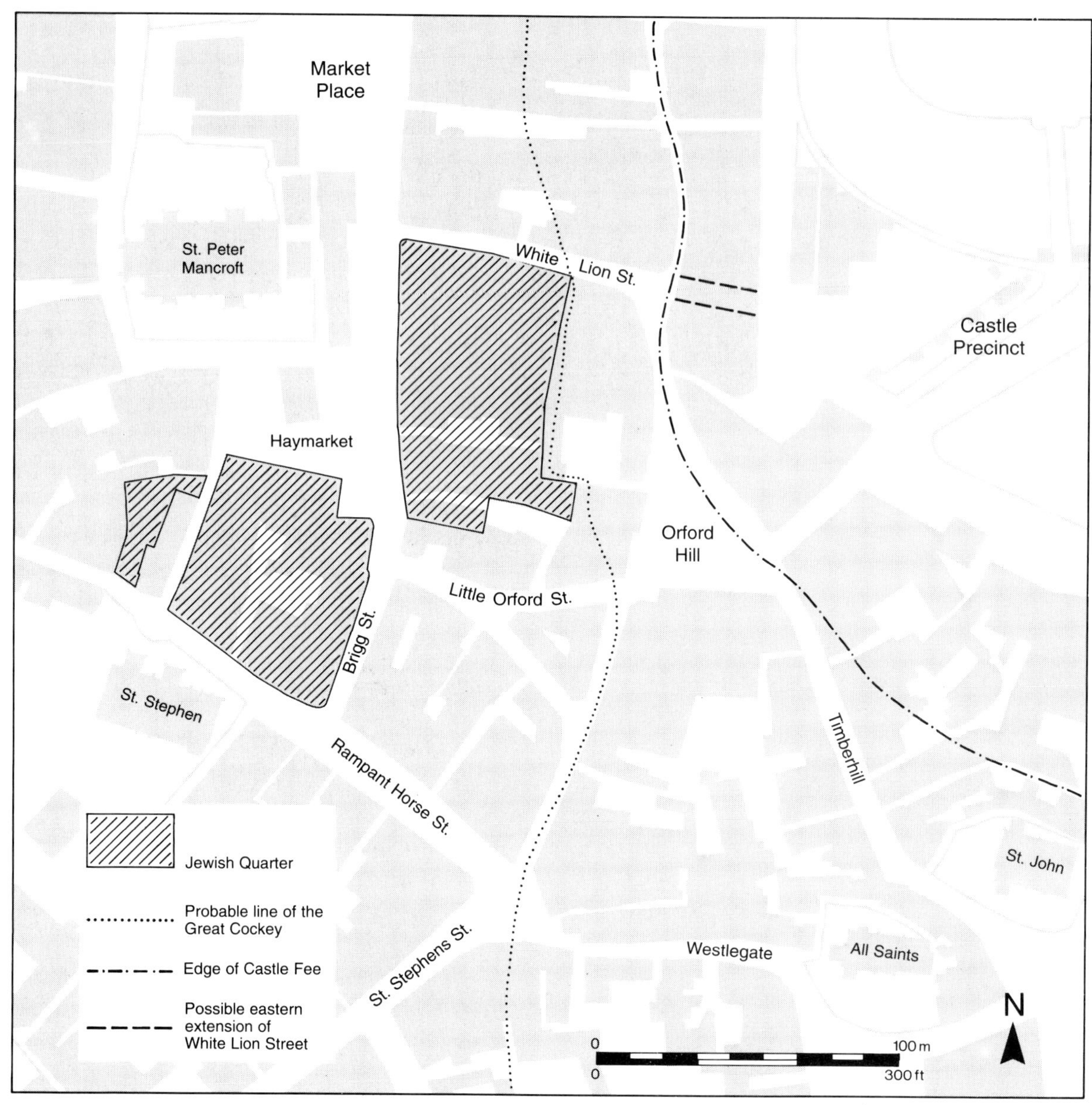

33 *Detail of the 1883 Ordnance Survey map annotated to show the edge of the Castle Fee, the medieval Jewish Quarter, a possible eastern extension of White Lion Street and the probable original line of the Great Cockey* (Ordnance Survey/Karen Guffogg after Lipman).

Jewish financier, and from him it passed to his son, Isaac. Isaac clearly used the river to trade as he was licensed to extend his staith behind the building in 1225.

Isaac's role as a financier ensured that he appears frequently in Exchequer records and one of these, dated 1233, contains a caricature of him together with his agent Mosse Mokke and a woman called Avegaye (**34**). This, perhaps the earliest caricature in England, depicts Isaac as the three-headed king of Norwich, its anti-semitic point nevertheless demonstrating his great importance.

34 *Anti-semitic cartoon on an Exchequer document of 1232–33 depicting Isaac, the son of Jurnet, and other Norwich Jews (*Public Record Office*).

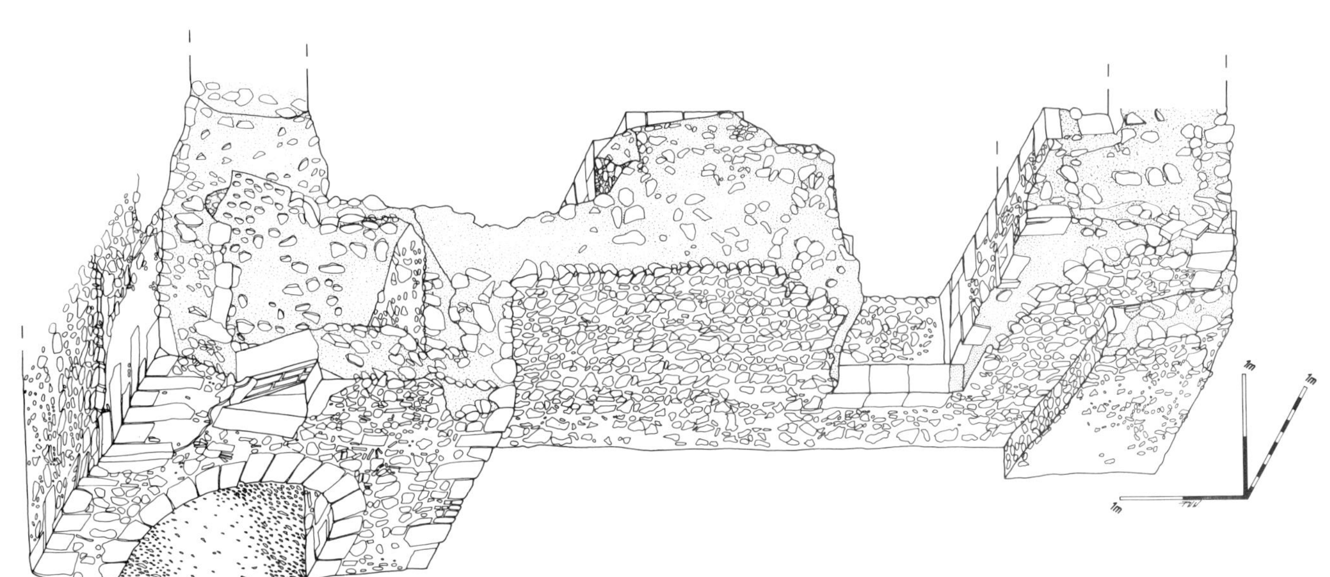

35 *Axonometric projection of the north-east corner of an excavated twelfth-century stone building on St Martin-at-Palace Plain, 1981. This building has been preserved beneath the new Magistrates' Courts (*Philip Williams*).

Buildings

The house of Jurnet and Isaac was not the only stone house in Norwich. Others are known from later documents when references were made to buildings such as the 'stonhus' in St Michael Conesford parish (also on King Street). These buildings were rare and appear to have been generally clustered in four principal areas: around the Market Place; along the waterfront on King Street; on Tombland (an eroded capital survives in the cellars of the Maid's Head Hotel); and along the waterfront north of the cathedral.

It is at this last location that a further stone building has now been discovered. Excavations in 1981 at St Martin-at-Palace Plain on the site of the new Magistrates' Courts unexpectedly revealed a twelfth-century building of flint rubble with limestone dressings (**35**). It stands (the ruin is preserved beneath the Courts in a modern basement) at right-angles to the street with internal measurements of 13.5m by 6.7m (44ft by 22ft). Cut into the hill, ground-floor access was afforded from the street to a first-floor hall, below which was a partly-cellared basement. This was served with two doorways

36 *Detail of the south window and later fifteenth-century corbels in the excavated stone building, St Martin-at-Palace Plain, 1981. The base of the brick vault is also visible (*Brian Ayers*).*

and three window openings (**36**) and seems to have been roofed in timber. At the northern (river) end of the building is a latrine turret, designed to allow the removal of effluent from the upper floor(s).

The nearest parallel for this excavated structure, both in terms of style and distance, is the Music House and the buildings are approximately contemporary. The excavated example was almost certainly a monastic property, attached to the Benedictine priory of the cathedral. Rents were payable to the cellarer of the cathedral, implying that the building may have been used as a victualling warehouse for the monastery. It was destroyed in the late thirteenth century, perhaps in 1272 when the townspeople rioted against the priory.

Urban development

The construction of the building took place on land acquired by the Bishop in 1106. The excavation revealed that the site had been occupied by earlier timber buildings but, following clearance in the mid-twelfth century, the area seems to have been laid out afresh, the stone building standing within a tenement plot some 18m (60ft) wide. Analysis of property boundaries on the 1883 Ordnance Survey map, together with a thirteenth-century list of the prior's landgable (rents on land), would suggest that the tenement of the stone building was only one of a number of similar tenements, each about 60ft wide. Each paid 1d in landgable, except for a narrower property next to St Martin's bridge some 30ft wide which paid a halfpenny. Parallel relationships between rent and tenement size are known from King's Lynn (also ecclesiastical land) where the 'new land' was laid out in the twelfth century. The implication for Norwich is one of town planning *de novo* on a site which was already in urban use.

Further plantation took place north of the river Wensum in the second quarter of the twelfth century. Here, on land west of Tolthorp Lane (subsequently Rattenrowe and Peacock Street) Eborard, the second bishop of Norwich, established a small community around the church and hospital of St Paul on land belonging to his manor of Thorpe. It is an area that has not been subject to excavation, save for small-scale work east of Whitefriars which indicates that its lowlying position meant that it was marginal land which needed considerable dumping of infilling deposits to ensure its viability. The episcopal initiative can hardly be called a success; the area was always to remain peripheral to the centres of activity in the growing city.

Planned expansion such as that around St Paul's church was complemented by more *ad hoc* expansion to both the north and south. Linear development along the line of Magdalen Street north of the Anglo-Scandinavian defences seems to have taken place at the end of the eleventh and the beginning of the twelfth century, with the church of St Margaret *in Combusto*, the most northerly church within the later walled city, being founded about 1100. Other churches to the north-west, such as St Augustine and St Martin-at-Oak, may have been founded at about the same time. This expansion was probably encouraged by the gradual decay, and ultimate removal, of the Anglo-Scandinavian defensive bank and ditch. These were perhaps outmoded before 1066 but would certainly have ceased to have any official function in the aftermath of the Conquest. Excavations at Alms Lane and Calvert Street indicate that the ditch was filled with rubbish or backfilled with its rampart around 1100.

South of the river, development extended along King Street in the early twelfth century. The area is again one which has not been subjected to detailed excavation but the indications are that settlement does not generally predate 1100 in that part of the street south of Mountergate. Even churches of apparent early date such as St Julian (with its round tower and 'basket' window) may be Norman in foundation, although it is possible that the churches of St Clement and St Etheldreda do indicate the location of pre-Conquest settle-ment. Development after 1100 does seem to have been reasonably intense, however, culminating in the construction of a number of stone houses including, of course, that of Jurnet.

Expansion was not possible to the east due to the location of the river and its marsh (and the land of the Bishop) but, to the west, development continued. Clay-walled structures of late twelfth-century date have been recognized from excavations in this area while the Late Saxon growth of St Benedict's Street seems to have been supplemented by development of the river marsh off Westwick Street, also in the twelfth century. This gradual encroachment on the river is characteristic of much of the central part of the city in this period, with infilling of the river margins occurring on both banks.

The growth of settlement on either side of the river probably necessitated the construction of additional bridges. It was noted above (p.00) that Fye Bridge was probably built before the Conquest, although the earliest known documentary reference is 1130–3 (a causeway structure of oak piles was observed in 1896 and a coin, possibly of William the Conqueror or William Rufus, found within it). St Martin's or Whitefriars Bridge was constructed by 1106 and may be pre-Conquest, but could have been erected to link the cathedral precinct to episcopal land north of the river. By the end of the twelfth century a third bridge existed, linking Oak Street with Coslany Street in the western part of the city. In the thirteenth century this bridge is referred to as 'duos pontes de Koselanye', probably because the bridge was in two parts, using an island in the river as a midway stage. The place-name 'Coslany' refers to such an island, which became attached to the north bank by infilling in later centuries.

Trade and industry

Riverside colonization seems to have been undertaken primarily for industrial reasons. Excavations at St Martin-at-Palace Plain located deposits of the first half of the twelfth century with considerable quantities of *Reseda luteola* seeds (dyer's rocket) being found in the soil samples, providing evidence for the nearby use of the plant in the dyeing process. Norwich was beginning to establish itself as a cloth-finishing city, probably working on cloth produced in the surrounding countryside although there is a curious reference in a French chronicle to the sack of Norwich in 1174 by the Flemings when the settlement failed to defend itself adequately as Norwich men were 'for the most part ... weavers, they know not to bear arms in knightly wise'. Weavers would have needed wool to make cloth and excavation in 1992 on Whitefriars recovered an early wool comb of bone, the first to be found in the city.

Tanning and skinning were other riverside trades, exploiting the hides of the increasing numbers of animals brought into the city for slaughter. Skinners probably worked on Mountergate and there is an early oblique reference to the trade in accounts of the life of St William of Norwich, the boy saint ostensibly murdered by the Jews about 1144. William was apprenticed to a skinner and therefore is the earliest recorded apprentice in English history.

Other industries along the river included hornworking, where cattle horns were steeped in pits full of urine and water to remove the tine; examples have been located on Pitt Street and on Fishergate. Hornworking also took place next to the streams or cockeys which flowed through the town; horn waste was recovered from the Midland Bank site on London Street next to the Great Cockey. Iron-working was practised on the river gravels. Excavations at Alms Lane north of the river in 1976 uncovered quarries for nodular ore or iron pan, roasting hearths and smelting furnaces. Mills stood in the western part of the city (the Westwick or Appleyard mills are recorded from 1175 and the 'Calk milnes' from about 1186).

Evidence for daily life in Norman Norwich continues to be located by excavation. The production of pottery in the town seems to have ceased by the mid twelfth century, but supplies of pottery were imported from the immediate hinterland and further afield. Commercial sites and affluent locations such as the castle reveal fragments of high quality Andenne ware from the Low Countries or Pingsdorf, a red-painted pottery from the Rhineland (a wine merchant from Cologne is mentioned in a document of 1144). Other continental imports include hone stones from Norway and quern stones from Germany, while occasional discoveries of pottery from Beauvais and Rouen suggest that the Norman Conquest brought an expansion to trade links which hitherto seem to have largely centred on the Rhine basin and the Baltic.

Environmental evidence

Less obvious imports were plants, introduced to England through ports such as Norwich.

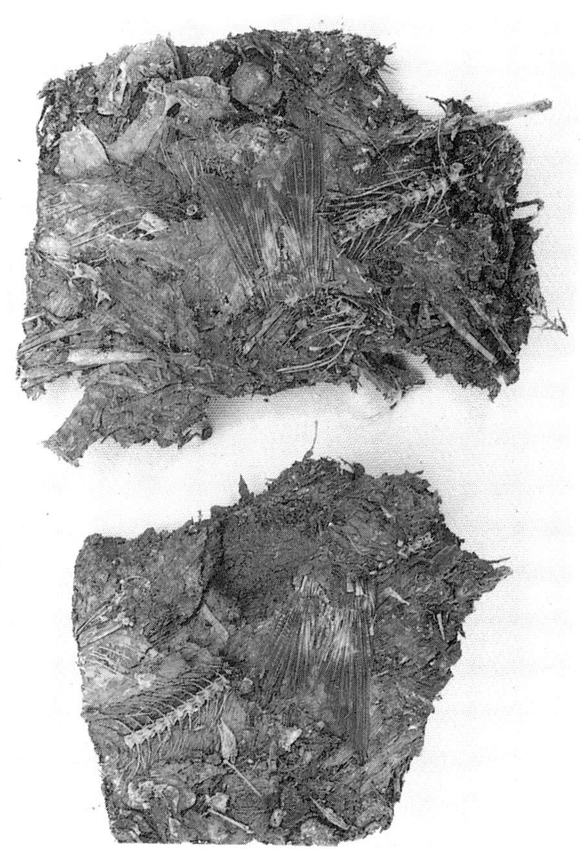

37 *Articulated fish bones, mainly of herring, recovered from the twelfth-century filling of a gully at St Martin-at-Palace Plain in 1981 (*Mick Sharp*).*

Analysis of microscopic seeds from Whitefriars has revealed the earliest known instances in the country of pot marigold and hops. Part of a walnut was also found, the earliest known post-Roman instance of the nut in England. Such discoveries help to develop a picture of a society which was both growing and outward looking.

Scientific analysis of microscopic flora and fauna, as well as the study of larger environmental ecofacts such as fish bone, also enables a clearer understanding of everyday life. Well-preserved organic deposits of late eleventh- and early twelfth-century date, excavated in 1981 near the river, provided excellent evidence for the content of midden or cess deposits. Cereals, cleansing waste, food refuse and floor sweepings of bracken and heather were all identified, as well as fruits such as sloe, bullace, plum, cherry, apple, strawberry, medlar, grape and elderberry. Fish remains were dominated by marine species, notably herring and cod (**37**). Animal bones consisted mainly of cattle, sheep and pig, although cats and dogs (presumably domestic pets but hounds were most probably kept as well) were also found, as well as occasional deer and hare. Diet, therefore, seems to have been as varied as local resources allowed.

Norwich by the end of the twelfth century was a considerably larger settlement than at the Conquest. It had been augmented by development on marginal land and along the river, notably to the south. Much of this development remains to be explored archaeologically (the Norman waterfront is only one area of great significance as yet untested by the trowel) but the broad trend of development seems clear. Norwich had consolidated its position as the most important settlement in the county, and indeed the region, assisted by a relative decline in both Thetford and Ipswich. It is likely that its status as a port was already threatened by Great Yarmouth in the twelfth century, but the diversification of industrial, commercial and administrative importance in Norwich was sufficiently advanced that wealth would continue to accumulate. This, however, was secular wealth; Norwich was also exceptionally important as a Norman ecclesiastical centre, an aspect of its development which needs to be explored in the next chapter.

38 *Composite comb of antler with iron rivets from Whitefriars Street, 1979, and double-sided comb from St Martin-at-Palace Plain, 1981.*

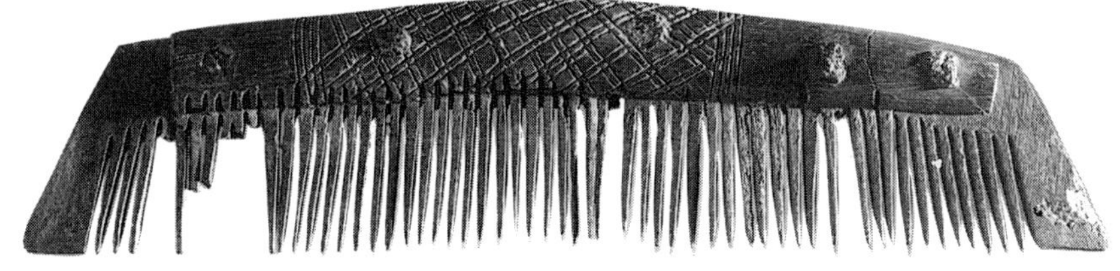
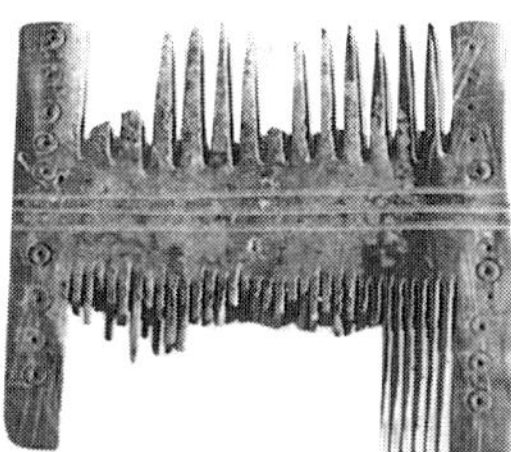

4

Norman Norwich –
the ecclesiastical town

The Normans almost certainly found Norwich to be a town of churches. It has been observed that a minimum of 25 were probably in existence by 1066 (p. 31) and that many of these churches were located on street corners of the Anglo-Saxon town (p. 34). Some, such as St Clement and St Gregory, were clearly extensive in influence, while others were held by great magnates such as the Abbots of Ely and Bury or the Archbishop of Canterbury himself.

Norwich in 1066, however, was not the seat of the bishopric, although the Bishop of East Anglia held land in the settlement including three-quarters of a mill, half an acre of meadow and a dwelling. The seat of the bishopric was at the rural site of Elmham; it was moved about 1072 by Bishop Herfast to Thetford in pursuit of final establishment at Bury St Edmunds. William the Conqueror granted a block of property in Norwich to Herfast, a grant of about 1075 recorded as follows in Domesday Book: '14 dwellings which King William gave to E(rfast) for the principal seat of the Bishopric...'. Herfast's claim to Bury was opposed by the abbot and the claim was abandoned in 1081 but the seat remained in Thetford.

Herbert de Losinga, created bishop in 1090, determined to move the seat to Norwich and this was effected from 1094. Land was acquired in stages, building on the Conqueror's original grant, with confirmation of 'the land of St Michael' sometime before 1100, the grant of the manor of Thorpe in 1101 (which included land west of the river, Thorpe itself lying to the east) and, in 1106, 'the land from the bishop's land to the water, and from the bridge of St Martin to the land of St Michael'. These grants formed the area now occupied by the Cathedral Close, together with land outside the Close that lay within the liberty of the bishopric.

Herbert was also empowered to augment the site of his episcopal seat with a Benedictine priory in a decree issued on Christmas Day 1100 by Henry I: 'in the church which is building...Herbert may place monks there who shall be irremoveable...'. The construction of the church seems to have started in 1096 and, like that of the castle, involved considerable destruction of the earlier Anglo-Saxon town. The destruction occurred after Domesday Book was compiled and thus is not recorded therein, but it is clear that the churches of St Michael Tombland and Holy Trinity were demolished and it is probable that entire streets of houses were also removed.

Norwich Cathedral

The cleared space was the site of a colossal building campaign. Construction of the great cathedral church, where work started at the east end, was accompanied by construction of a palace for the bishop to the north and the monastic buildings of the priory to the south. In addition, a convent wall was built around

39 *Creation of a new access doorway through part of the north nave aisle exterior wall in 1988 showing the flint core of the Cathedral church fabric with ashlar internal and external facings (*Kirk Laws-Chapman*).*

40 *Excavations at the east end of the Cathedral church in 1931 revealing the foundations of the late eleventh-century apse (*Norfolk and Norwich Archaeological Society*).*

of the building are constructed in flint rubble with lime mortar. A section through the north wall of the north nave aisle was observed in 1988 (**39**).

There has been little archaeological excavation in and around the church, other than for observations during remedial works and limited investigations at the west end and adjacent to the north transept. A major excavation was undertaken in 1930–31, however, by Dean Cranage, prior to the construction of a new chapel on the site of the destroyed Lady Chapel. This unearthed evidence for the original eastern apse of the building (**40**), complementing semicircular side chapels which survive, and confirming the plan of the cathedral as one based upon the Cluniac ideal of a church with an ambulatory around and behind the altar.

It is this plan which has inspired what is perhaps the most interesting archaeological detective work of recent years concerning the church and its associated buildings. While the orientation of the church is east to west (and possibly overlies directly the line of east to west

the close and gates were erected. The eastern end of the church, together with the transepts, tower and four bays of nave west of the tower, were completed by Herbert's death in 1119. His successor, Eborard, is said to have completed the church by the 1140s ('*ecclesiam integraliter consummavit*') but the final consecration took place as late as 1278.

Despite alterations and depredations during the last 900 years, significant quantities of Norman work remain. The church itself is the greatest single survivor, with the nave, transepts, tower and presbytery being substantially Norman (except for the roofs and the clerestory of the presbytery). Although faced largely in Caen or Barnack limestone, the walls

Holme Street, the Roman road), analysis of the structure has convinced Professor Fernie that, mathematically, the layout of the building was conceived using the principle of one to the square root of two. This principle extended to a determination of the layout of the cloister and of the orientation of the bishop's palace.

Both cloister and palace contain much original Norman work. The cloister was badly damaged in a riot of 1272 and its public face was rebuilt in perpendicular style, but internally much Norman blind arcading is visible, as are the distinctive interior windows of the refectory to the south. West of the cloister was a guest wing (with so-called 'Saxon' basket windows) while the dormitory, reredorter and chapter house lay to the east.

The palace was originally linked to the north aisle of the nave but was 'disjoined' in the 1850s. Although grievously converted to school use in 1858–9, substantial traces of Norman work survive, including a vaulted undercroft and, masked by later additions, what is essentially the earliest (and smallest) tower keep in Norfolk. Part of the palace overlies an earlier graveyard, possibly that of the Late Saxon church of Holy Trinity or Christ Church. Burials were observed running beneath the palace footings in 1960.

The Bishop and his prior stressed the links of the new church with the ancient seat of the bishopric by transferring the remains of the Saxon bishop's throne to a new site behind the high altar. The much damaged fragments of this throne survive, as does an effigy which was purpose-built for a niche above the exterior doorway to the north transept. This effigy, probably the earliest post-Roman large-scale figurative sculpture in England, was once thought to represent Bishop Herbert. It is now more generally felt to depict St Felix, who converted East Anglia to Christianity. Such a representation probably provided further emphasis of links with the past and legitimized the translation of the seat of the bishopric to its new location.

Links between the monastic precinct and the earlier town were provided by the continued existence of pre-Conquest churches within the Close. Not all were destroyed to clear the area and the churches of St Ethelbert, St Helen and St Mary-in-the-Marsh continued in use. St Helen was demolished about 1249 when the parish was amalgamated with the newly-founded Great Hospital, and St Ethelbert was destroyed in a riot of 1272. St Mary, however, survived as a church into the sixteenth century. It appears to have been rebuilt in the twelfth century; parts of the building still exist, its north wall providing the spine wall of Nos 10–12 The Close.

Most of the walls enclosing the cathedral

41 *Interior of the north side of the Ethelbert Gate showing the late eleventh-century flint walls, the original quoins damaged by fire in 1272, and part of the early fourteenth-century vault above the enlarged gateway (Brian Ayers).*

precinct also survive and, while much repair work has been undertaken, late eleventh-century and twelfth-century elements clearly still stand. One such element can be observed within the Ethelbert Gate, which leads out of the Close into the southern part of Tombland (**41**). The original gate was destroyed in 1272, but its successor was created by reusing much of the Norman gateway and walls. In consequence, parts of the precinct wall of *c*. 1100 can still be seen, as can quoins which probably formed the jambs of the interior gateway. These quoins retain distinctive Norman diagonal tooling, as well as fire damage probably sustained in 1272.

Water access to the precinct was facilitated by the construction of a canal from the river Wensum to the lower Close. Traditionally it is asserted that this was effected to allow ease of transport for stone to the cathedral and tradition may well be correct, although presumably it also provided the bishop and the prior with their own quay and thus they could avoid tolls. The canal could still be used in the eighteenth century; a keel or wherry is depicted upon a prospect of the city drawn in the 1720s sailing up to the cathedral. It was a 'stinking ditch' by the mid-nineteenth century, however, and was backfilled.

The canal was well placed to facilitate the movement of stone shipments reaching Norwich from the coast, but it was also sited opposite stone quarries on the east bank of the river Wensum. These quarries, traces of which still exist, were located at the foot of a steep hill leading up on to Mousehold Heath and must have been exploited for the vast quantities of flint and lime which were needed. They were within the manor of Thorpe and thus on episcopal land, standing on either side of the Roman road from Brundall. Exploitation took a different form in later centuries; in 1771 Sylas Neville, waiting for a chaise outside the city gate, 'found three curious Fossils, worth at least 15 shillings'. This consoled him for the expense of the chaise!

The ecclesiastical manor of Thorpe also pro-vided timber, of which the cathedral and its associated building would have required great quantities. Bishop Herbert was aware of the precious nature of this resource and, about 1100, issued orders for effective conservation of Thorpe Wood.

Other monastic foundations

At the top of the steep hill to the Heath, on the southern side of the road, was another monastic institution, St Leonard's Priory. This was also founded by Bishop Herbert, reputedly before the foundation of the cathedral. It was served by monks from the cathedral and little now survives, although there are fragmentary ruins among private gardens. The monks also served a small chapel to the north of the road. This was dedicated to St Michael and was built by Herbert in recompense for his destruction of the important pre-Conquest church of St Michael on Tombland. Most of this has also been destroyed, although a large section of the north wall still stands, constructed in courses of well-sorted cobbles.

Herbert de Losinga was clearly an energetic man, for, not content with the cathedral precinct, St Leonard's Priory, St Michael's Chapel and new churches in both Lynn and Yarmouth, he also founded two hospitals. One of these was dedicated to St Mary Magdalen and it stood to the north of the city on what is now Sprowston Road. This hospital, which became known as the Lazar House because of its associations with lepers (although it does not seem to have been exclusively for their use), was furnished with its own graveyard and chapel. Burials from the graveyard were recorded during construction works of the adjacent Gilman Road, some of them exhibiting leprosy in the bone. The chapel survives, converted to a public library. It has two decorated doorways and may originally have had a third (**42**).

The other foundation of Bishop Herbert seems to have been that of St Paul's, or Norman's Hospital. This stood to the north of the river (within the city), linked to the south

42 *The west door of the Lazar House, the restored chapel of the early twelfth-century Magdalen Hospital now used as a branch library, Sprowston Road (*Brian Ayers*).*

bank and to the Close by a bridge, that of St Martin. It occupied land which was part of the episcopal manor of Thorpe and therefore came within the liberty of the cathedral rather than that of the city. The area was lowlying and was probably situated immediately east of the eastern arm of the Anglo-Scandinavian defences. Here the second bishop, Eborard, completed the hospital which was linked with the parochial church of St Paul. Although it occupied a large area and was generously endowed by patrons (including the king), nothing now remains. It is possible that a later medieval wall uncovered in excavations at the eastern perimeter of the site in 1992 may represent part of its precinct wall. St Paul's church has also been destroyed, in its case by enemy action in 1942.

The Prior's Fee

The lands acquired by the bishop, on both banks of the river, passed into the control of the prior, with the Prior's Fee being exempt, like the castle, from city dues and taxation. The rights and privileges of the prior were to cause problems with the citizens for centuries. Investigation of the Prior's Fee continues to cause problems to the present day.

Primarily this is due to a lack of opportunity for archaeological work. The largest single area is that of the Cathedral precinct and this is generally free of development pressure. Intervention is therefore confined to small-scale excavation or watching-brief work. It is correspondingly difficult to chart the development of the Close through the buried archaeological record, although significant strides have been made with architectural and archaeological analysis of standing buildings. These studies suggest that there may be even more Norman work surviving within parts of the Close than is generally realized. In particular it is likely that the granary vaults date from the twelfth century, as does part of the building on the site of the Prior's boathouse.

Outside the Close, some archaeological and historical work has been undertaken on the Fee. It was noted above (p. 50) that work on St Martin-at-Palace Plain indicated that the area was laid out afresh in the twelfth century, almost certainly as a result of ecclesiastical intervention. The excavated stone building paid rents to the cellarer of the cathedral and it is also known that the cellarer took rents from a further stone house immediately outside the Ethelbert Gate on Tombland. The area of St Paul's church and hospital, however, together with the seventeen or so houses known to have been built nearby, remains largely unexplored.

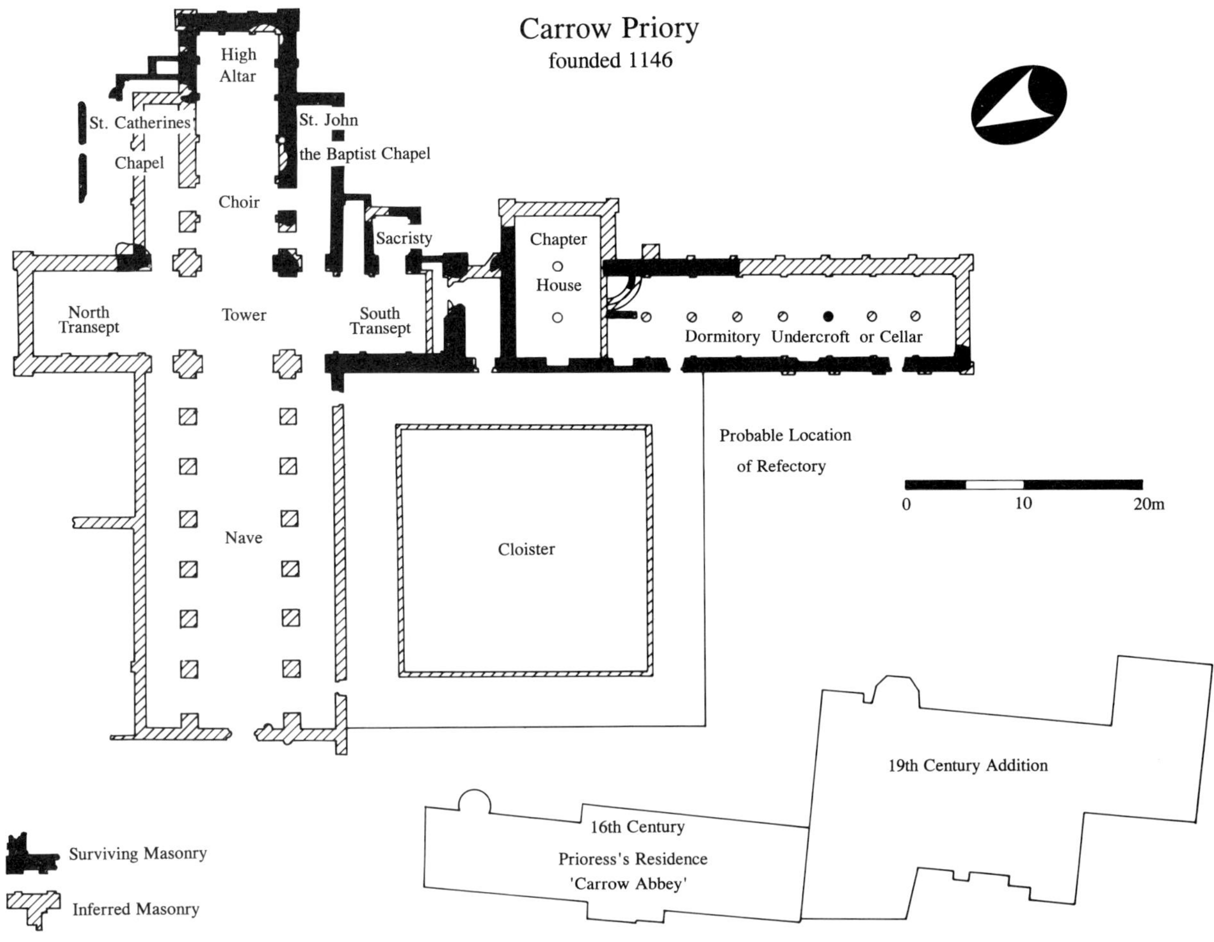

43 *Plan of Carrow Priory (*Piers Wallace*).*

Churches

The foundation of the church of St Paul indicates that church foundation did not stop with the Norman Conquest. Indeed it seems likely that the great market church of St Peter Mancroft was founded before 1075 and was probably the church held by the priest Wala in 1086. This was a foundation by a lay lord, Earl Ralph de Guader, and in this it seems to have continued a pre-Conquest tradition of the establishment of churches as proprietary churches or *Eigenkirchen* by individuals. Similarly, the church of St Giles was reputedly founded in the Conqueror's reign by Elwyn the priest on his own estate.

Other churches probably founded in the late eleventh or early twelfth century include St George Colegate and St George Tombland. St George, a popular dedication after the First Crusade of 1096, was probably given to a new church on Colegate as occupation expanded westwards along the north bank of the river in the twelfth century, linking the (once-fortified) area around Magdalen Street with the early nucleus of occupation at the southern end of Oak Street. St George Tombland appears to be an encroachment on Tombland, the site of the pre-Conquest market place, where commercial importance had been eclipsed by the establishment of a new market area in the

Norman borough. Construction of St George also seems to have blocked partially the alignment of the east to west Roman road (much of which had already been destroyed by the building of the cathedral), necessitating a bend in the line of Princes Street and, possibly, also leading to the establishment of the right-of-way through the churchyard which acts as a 'remembrance' of the lost road.

It is also possible to reconstruct probable topographical details from the position of St George Colegate or, rather, its parish boundary. St George seems to have been carved out of the earlier large parish of St Clement, and the boundary between the two parishes south of Colegate runs directly towards the river before veering eastwards. This is paralleled to the west by the line of Water Lane, which also runs directly south from Colegate before veering westwards. The effect is one of a funnel on the north bank of the river Wensum and it has been suggested that the boundary and lane may mark the edges of the original outflow of the Muspole stream (**44**).

This hypothesis was tested by a very small excavation in 1986 behind buildings on St George's Street (which now links Colegate to the river between the parish boundary and Water Lane). This discovered deep deposits of infilled material at a point 94m (300ft) north of the river, suggesting that the hypothesis may be correct. The infilling itself could date from the twelfth century as a further church, St Margaret Newbridge, is known to have stood off St George's Street near the river by 1157. The 'new bridge' itself is recorded by 1257 although this too could be a Norman innovation. After 1359 the church was converted to a hermitage chapel with the hermit having charge of the bridge.

Another church dedicated to St Margaret was that of St Margaret *in Combusto* at the northern end of Magdalen Street. Although this church ceased to function in the fifteenth century, and was probably demolished in the sixteenth century, the site has been excavated

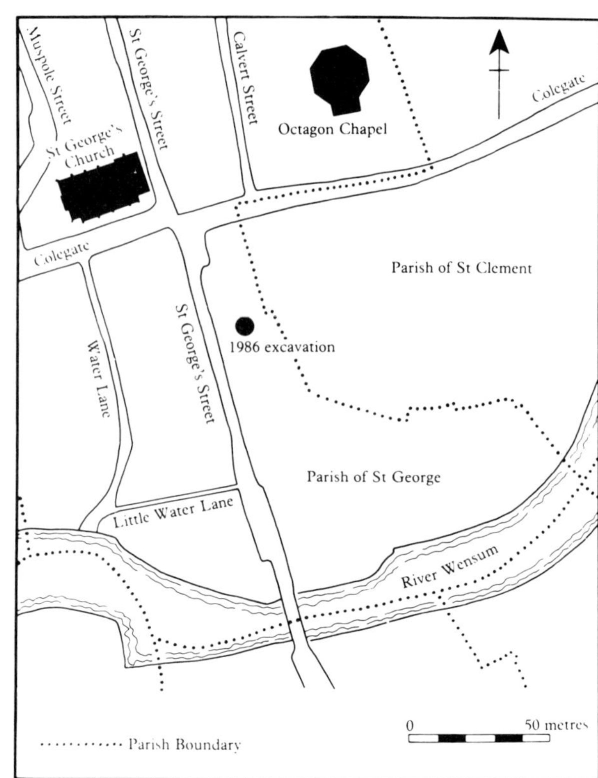

44 *Map showing Water Lane and the boundary between the parishes of St Clement and St George. These possibly indicate the edges of the original outflow of the Muspole. Subsequent infilling allowed the establishment of the southern part of St George's Street (*Jayne Bown*).*

(in 1987). Remains of the building had been comprehensively destroyed by the cellars of a nineteenth-century Blind Institute, but a large part of the graveyard was uncovered. This came into use about 1100 and clearly served an impoverished parish. Over 430 skeletons were recovered, some of whom appear to have been the victims of plague or other infectious diseases. Analysis of the bones is continuing but it is hoped that the results will enable comparison with the pre-Conquest group from the Anglia Television site (pp. 37–8) and thereby provide data on the continued development of the population of Norwich.

No memorials were discovered at St Margaret and these are indeed uncommon until late in the Middle Ages. A memorial stone of twelfth-century date was reused in the city wall, however, near the King Street Gate. It was recovered in 1924 and has a Latin inscription seeking prayers for the soul of Bertrand de Fun . . . eki (the name is partly indecipherable). It is not known which graveyard it came from although the nearest would have been that of St Peter Southgate, a church in existence by the last quarter of the twelfth century.

Partial excavation has also been undertaken in another Norman church, that of St James. The earliest documentary reference to this parish is 1180. Limited work during conversion of the church building to a puppet theatre in 1979 revealed that the earliest phase of the structure consisted of an aisleless nave with a long narrow chancel built of roughly-knapped flint. A number of fragments of twelfth-century architectural detailing were also recovered (**45**), including sections of Romanesque colonnette shafts and voussoir blocks with diamond lozenges and spiked foliate decoration. The stone is Caen, suggesting a possible link with the Cathedral Priory, although the bishop did not take control of the living until 1201. The church stood, however, on episcopal land with a parish which extended out of the growing city into the surrounding areas of Pockthorpe and Mousehold Heath (also episcopal land).

Other churches can be suggested as Norman foundations such as St Michael-at-Thorn (destroyed by bombing in 1942) and St Julian (also bombed but rebuilt). The site of St Michael is now used as a surface car park but it would clearly repay excavation should development take place, especially as it had a Norman doorway. This was salvaged after the Second World War and transferred to the rebuilt St Julian. Here, the round tower and 'basket' windows are often taken to indicate pre-Conquest origin, but the foundation could date as easily to the late eleventh or early twelfth century.

Twelfth-century foundations

A further Norman creation was that of St William's chapel upon Mousehold Heath to the east of the city. The boy William was murdered in 1144, was subsequently canonized and a shrine established in the cathedral. The site of the discovery of his body was marked by the construction of a chapel, earthworks of which remain.

The largest Norman church of Norwich after the cathedral, however, was that of the priory at Carrow (immediately south of the city). This was founded about 1146 as a Benedictine nunnery and grew rapidly to become one of the largest and most important such houses in the country. Ruins still stand, notably of the cloister and the Prioress's lodgings, but also of the dormitory undercroft, the chapter house, slype and the church itself.

Excavations prior to consolidation in 1981 revealed remains of tiled floors dating from the twelfth to the fifteenth centuries and nine graves of adult females. The plan as visible was largely excavated in 1881. The church was 60m (195ft) in length with a rectangular chancel and transepts with chapels. A complete thirteenth-century jar recovered in 1968 (with an inscription apparently ADAM) may have been used as an

45 *Decorated stone from the church of St James, 1979 showing the eagle of St John the Evangelist (*Norwich Survey*).*

acoustic jar in one of the priory walls. The priory stood on a low rise between the Wensum and Yare valleys and must have dominated the confluence of these two rivers and the downstream approach to Norwich.

The Norman legacy to Norwich, therefore, is very great. Ecclesiastical foundations and secular institutions, together with a major expansion of the area of settlement, produced a city of the first rank by the end of the twelfth century. It is a city where archaeological exploration, both above and below ground, continues to reveal evidence of Norman activity. Norwich received its first charter in the reign of Henry II but it is the 1194 charter of Richard I, at the end of the Norman period, that best characterizes the emerging nature of the settlement. This enabled the citizens to elect their own reeve instead of being governed by a royal official. Norwich was ceasing to be a mere borough and was emerging as a great medieval city.

5

Norwich before the Black Death

It is possible to reconstruct a map of Norwich on the eve of the Black Death (1349) which depicts a city of extraordinary size and complexity (**46**). An urban area some $1^1/_2$ miles from north to south and 1 mile from east to west, bounded by a defensive wall and ditch on three sides, stands on both banks of the river Wensum which is itself crossed by no fewer than five bridges. Within the defended area is a royal castle, a Benedictine monastery and cathedral, four large friary precincts, several hospitals, nearly sixty parish churches, a commercial waterfront, warehouses, markets, houses of an affluent merchant class and homes of the urban poor. The city is larger in area than London and Southwark combined and, although its population is inferior to that of London, at about 30,000 is still exceptional for the Middle Ages.

This great city was a product of the development described in the foregoing chapters. The consolidation of this development – building upon the city's role as a market, an industrial centre, a port and an administrative centre (both secular and ecclesiastical) – was essentially a phenomenon of the thirteenth century. At this period it is possible to view the city emerging as a cohesive unit, with citizens who were consciously seeking to extend the liberties of Norwich.

City walls

The most tangible reminder of this idea, that of promoting the city as its own entity, survives today in the ruins of the city wall. Work started on a communal defensive system, which also defined the city and allowed control of trade, in 1253. A bank was erected with upcast material from a ditch and, presumably, a timber revetment was set on top of the bank. The ditch cut through the prior's land at Pockthorpe on the north bank of the river, an assertion of the citizens' power which raised strong objection from the ecclesiastic authorities.

The first murage grant, enabling a masonry wall to be built, was made in 1297. The complete circuit was not finished until 1344 and, even then, was only achieved when a wealthy private citizen, Richard Spynk, paid for considerable stretches out of his own purse. There were over 40 towers and 12 gates, using prodigious quantities of flint and mortar. Boom towers were erected at the southern end where the wall met the river, enabling a chain of Spanish iron to be stretched across the Wensum to inhibit river traffic.

The gates were all pulled down between 1791 and 1810, although it is possible to gain an impression of them from a series of eighteenth-century engravings (**47**). The south side of St Benedict's Gate survived until 1942, complete with a doorpin, but this ruin was destroyed in the 'Baedeker' air raid of April that year. None of the gates has been excavated. Foundations of St Stephen's Gate, the main gate to London and Ipswich, were uncovered during the con

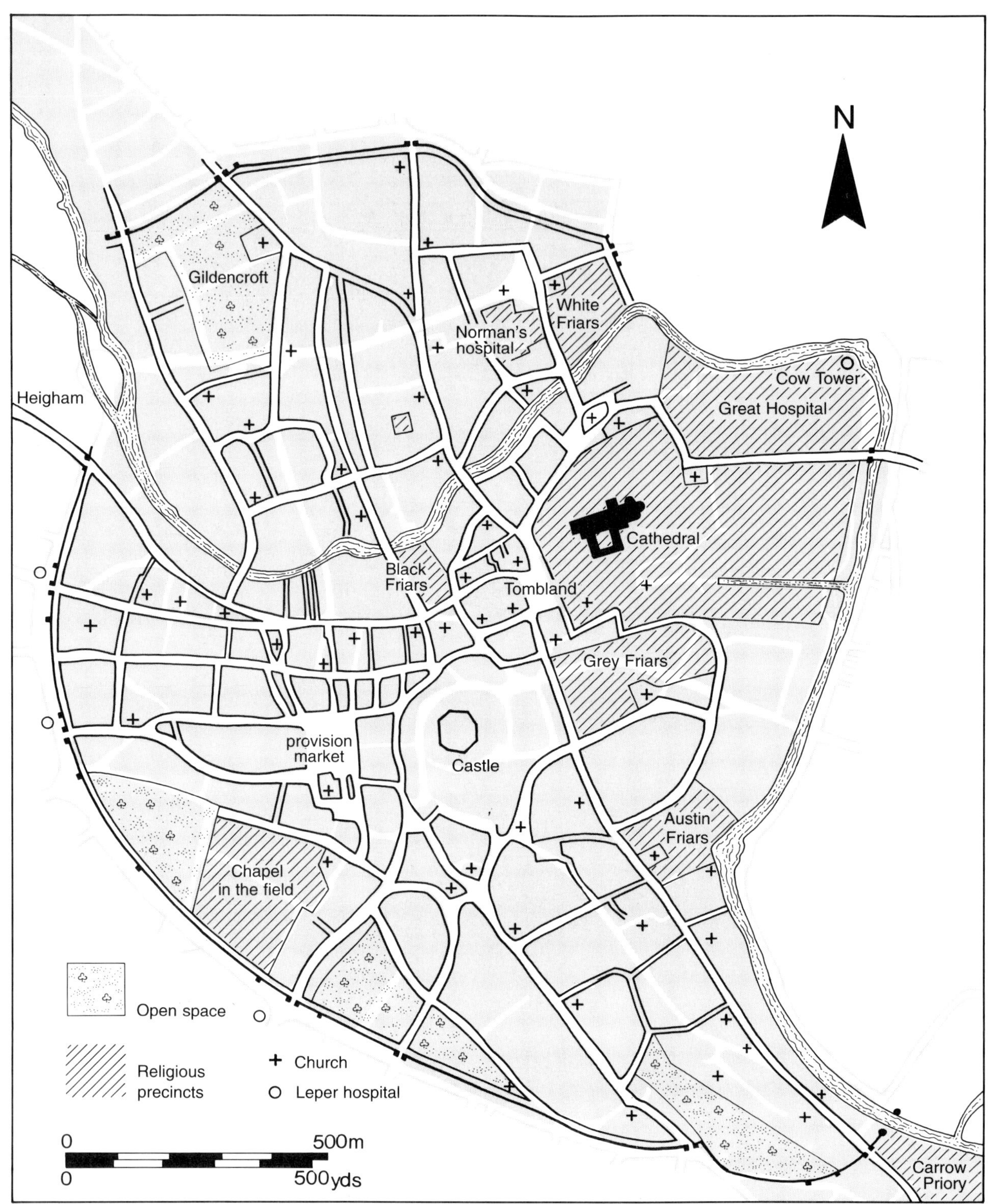

46 *Map of the medieval city in the mid fourteenth century* (Karen Guffogg).

1   *Air view of an Anglo-Saxon cemetery at Caistor St. Edmund on the line of the Norwich southern bypass. At least 45 people were buried during the late seventh/early eighth centuries, a small number of them accompanied by gold and silver jewellery. The cemetery lies immediately south of the remains of a round barrow constructed about 1700 BC (Derek Edwards, Norfolk Landscape Archaeology)*

2   *Excavation of the barbican gatehouse well, Norwich Castle 1991. The well was dug in stages, as redevelopment removed the surrounding deposits. It and the gatehouse stood at the foot of the bridge to the mound (top left), inside a massive ditch (Neil Moss)*

3   Air view of Norwich Cathedral Close (Derek Edwards, Norfolk Landscape Archaeology)

4   Excavation of a probable masons' yard, Norwich Cathedral 1987, visible as an area of limestone chippings and sawdust. The view is taken from the roof of the north transept (Martin Smith)

5   *The view south of the remains of the dormitory undercroft east of the cloister at
Carrow Priory (Kirk Laws-Chapman)*

6 *Back of Magdalen Gates, Norwich 1809 by Robert Dixon. The title is a later one and the picture actually depicts a tower which stands at the junction of Barrack Street with Silver Road (Norfolk Museums Service, Norwich Castle Museum)*

7   The church of St Peter Mancroft, rebuilt between 1430 and 1455 (Brian Ayers)

8   Reconstruction of the interior of a clay-walled building at Alms Lane (Martin Creasey/Norwich Survey)

9   (Below) Reconstruction of Norwich Castle from the west showing the barbican gate. Archaeological excavation at Castle Mall suggested that access to the Castle may have been effected from the west at an early period, providing a link with the Market Place via White Lion Street, although such a route was blocked by the later Middle Ages (Nick Arber/Norfolk Museums Service)

10   (Right) The Cow Tower next to the River Wensum, a late fourteenth-century freestanding artillery fortification of flint with brick facing (Brian Ayers)

11   (Far right) Interior of Dragon Hall, King Street, showing the mid-fifteenth-century crown post roof (Kirk Laws-Chapman)

*12   St James' Mill, Whitefriars, 'the most noble of all English Industrial Revolution mills'
(Brian Ayers)*

47 *Interior of the Magdalen Gate prior to demolition, originally drawn by John Kirkpatrick in the eighteenth century and redrawn by Henry Ninham in 1860 (Norfolk Museums Service, Norwich Castle Museum).*

struction of underpasses for the Inner Ring Road in 1964. A sketch plan is the only known record.

The walls and towers have also suffered grievously but considerable stretches still stand. Excavation has been limited save for work on Barn Road in 1948 and 1954 which uncovered the early bank, a ditch that was 4 m (12ft) deep, 20m (60ft) wide and wet at this location, and a semicircular projecting turret, trenches on Queen's Road in 1962–3 which revealed traces of an upcast gravel bank and a minor excavation north of the Wensum in 1987 at River Lane. This uncovered the foundations of the wall in an area where it approaches the river, and the threshold and door jamb of the turret which stood next to the river. These details were fashioned in brick, although the wall and turret themselves were built of flint. The River Lane stretch appears to be a late addition to the circuit, possibly of *c.* 1377.

The wall was built in courses of flint which, because of the large quantities of mortar necessary, had to be erected in 'lifts', each lift of between 0.3m (1ft) and 0.5m (20in) in height being shuttered and allowed to set before the next 'lift' was added. It is often possible to detect such 'lifts' in the surviving stretches of wall. The full height of the wall was some 4m (12ft), the only surviving part at this height being next to the site of the Ber Street Gate where (much restored) battlements can be seen finished in brick.

The exterior face of the wall was frequently built in front of an arcade which supported the wall-walk. This arcade survives in several places with the recesses within the arcade acting as embrasures for the arrow loops. The Carrow Hill section provides a good example (**48**). At Barn Road, the face of the wall has been removed but the arcade stands as a series of arches.

The wall-walk passed through the interval towers, doorways being extant at the Black Tower on Carrow Hill and on the tower next to the site of St Stephen's Gate. This tower retains part of its brick vault above which the wall-walk passes. It also has the remains of two gunloops for primitive artillery, probably among the earliest such loops in the country. A smaller loop, for a hand gun, survives in the stretch of wall between this tower and the gate. Other loops are known elsewhere, notably at Baker Road, where a particularly fine example survives, fashioned in limestone rather than brick.

Parts of the circuit were served by lanes immediately inside the wall, providing ease of access. St Martin-at-Oak Wall Lane, Wellington Lane and Bull Lane are surviving examples.

The exceptionally large circuit of the defences encompassed most of the existing built-up area in the fourteenth century, although it excluded the hamlet of Heigham which thereafter developed as a small western suburb. The great

48 *Arcade on the interior of the City Wall at Carrow Hill to support the parapet walk (Brian Ayers).*

sweep of wall necessitated the enclosure of open spaces as well, in order to reduce awkward salients, and some of these to the north and west remained open space into the eighteenth and nineteenth centuries (such as Gildencroft, 12 acres of land inside the north-western stretch of the walls which included a 'Justing Acre'). The defended area also included the commercial waterfront on King Street, which seems to have been thriving by the thirteenth century. The southern end of the street in particular was busy: references are made to St Julian's Staith in 1275, Frankestathe in 1290 and St Olave's Staith in 1346.

Waterfront

There has not been any excavation on this waterfront, so the potential for increasing understanding of the commercial role of Norwich at this period remains unquantified. Small-scale excavation has taken place within a building on the King Street frontage next to St Julian's Staith. This revealed slight evidence for twelfth-century timber structures followed by the construction of late thirteenth- or early fourteenth-century buildings with ground-floor flint-rubble walls. These walls survive, reused to support a major rebuilding campaign in the fifteenth century.

Riverside activity continued upstream as well. Rushworth's Staith is recorded in 1291, probably near the outflow of the Dallingfleet stream into the river Wensum immediately south of the Cathedral Close. Much riverside shipment here must have been associated with the Cathedral Priory, not least supplying it with the hundreds of thousands of peat turves which it burnt for fuel each year by the early fourteenth century.

North of the Close, however, it is likely that wharfage facilities were reserved for small fishing craft or boats serving riverside industries. St Edmund's Quay off Fishergate may well have been used by fishermen in the twelfth and thirteenth centuries (a large anchor was reputedly found during the digging of a cellar in the parish of St Edmund in 1686) although the available documentation would suggest that, by the early fourteenth century, the river frontage had largely been taken over by skinners, tanners, fullers and dyers.

Fishing was important, nevertheless: herring pies were tendered to the Crown in the thirteenth century and had probably been offered earlier. Many fishermen were concentrated in the parish of St George Tombland, close to the cathedral, where a fish house is recorded in 1272. Another fish house is mentioned on Quayside in 1286; this belonged to Maud or Matilda of Catton who had blocked Quayside when she had it built. Shellfish were landed further west on Quayside. Rapid salvage excavation in 1963 beneath the site of the New Star Inn uncovered a layer of oyster shells 0.46m (18in) thick.

Trade and industry

The gradual colonization of the river foreshore by industry is particularly notable from the thirteenth century. Analysis of documents, especially the Enrolled Deeds (of 1285–1311, with later examples) has enabled a broad understanding of the disposition of craft industries throughout the city. This is particularly true of clothworkers such as dyers. These seem to have occupied the foreshore throughout the central part of the city although there was a distinct grouping of such workers in the Westwick Street area. The eastern part of Westwick Street was called Letestere Row (that is, Listers' or Dyers' Row) and it led to the Maddermarket where dyestuffs were sold (woad was imported from Amiens and Corbie after 1286). Two-thirds of the dyers mentioned in the Enrolled Deeds seem to have worked in this area.

Fullers were also cloth finishers who needed access to water and they were located close to the main group of dyers. All ten fullers mentioned in the Enrolled Deeds were in the western part of the city, as was 'Le Fulleres holes', a lane running to the river downstream of the dyers. Fullers needed clean water and it is difficult to see how this could be provided at Fullers Hole. A little further east was 'Bleckstershole', recorded from 1292, where the bleachers of woollen cloth worked. They also needed water and thus, with their colleagues the dyers and fullers, formed a considerable area of cloth finishing. They were joined by shearmen, who trimmed the nap on the cloth, and who occupied Shearing or Charing Cross between Letestere Row, Fullers Hole, Bleckstershole and the Maddermarket.

Although the cloth finishing trade was clearly important, the largest single industrial group in the city seems to have been that of the leatherworkers. These comprised skinners, tanners, tawyers, whitawyers, shoemakers, saddlers and parchment makers. The skinners, tanners and tawyers were most active next to the river, particularly in Conesford in the southern part of the city, but they were also working next to the streams which ran into the Wensum such as the Great Cockey and, probably, Barkeres (that is tanners') Fleet.

Archaeological evidence for the activities of these workers is slight, primarily because few areas of Norwich contain waterlogged deposits which preserve organic material and, to date, the number of excavations on river frontages is limited. Fragments of shoes in thirteenth-century contexts were recovered at St Martin-at-Palace Plain in 1981 but more detailed discoveries await the opportunity of greater excavation.

Increased colonization of the river foreshore, and the larger numbers of people living on both banks of the river, probably necessitated the construction of a further bridge, New Bridge, by 1257. This brought to four the number of bridges across the river in the city centre, greatly in excess of bridge provision in any other medieval English city, and five in total as the early crossing point east of the Cathedral Close, previously a ford on the line of the Roman road, was bridged about 1250. This bridge crossed the line of the defences as formed by the river and was therefore built with a gate tower about 1345. It is the only surviving medieval river bridge in the city, although its gate was demolished in 1791.

The riverside industries were complemented by other industries throughout the city. The Enrolled Deeds also mention goldsmiths, smiths, cutlers, lorimers (harness makers), latoners (brass workers), bell-founders, tailors, glovers, hatters, hosiers, girdlers, masons, carpenters, painters, roofers, coopers and boatmen among a total of some 68 different trades and services. Archaeological evidence for the products of these industries can be seen in the knives and padlocks recovered from excavations, in the remains of barrels often reused to line pits or in the walls of surviving thirteenth- and fourteenth-century structures (notably the defences).

Locally produced goods were supplemented by imports, and documents and archaeological excavation combine to illustrate the range of Norwich's trade contacts. Building stone came from France, material from Caen being transhipped in Yarmouth in 1288–9. Wine was brought from the Rhineland and, occasionally, from Gascony (sherds of Saintonge pottery, rare in Norwich, were found at the Magistrates' Courts site in 1981 and in the Greyfriars' precinct in 1993). Steel was imported from Sweden and silks from Italy. Everyday pottery was also imported; the city was served with the products of east Norfolk kilns as well as the major west Norfolk industry centred on Pott Row, Grimston. Vast quantities of these types, as well as more exotic vessels, are located on excavations.

The diversity of goods available for sale, as well as the range of services which a great urban centre needed to provide, ensured that the market system was equally diverse. By the thirteenth century there were specialist markets at All Saints Green (swine, replaced by timber), Orford Hill (swine), Rampant Horse Street (horses – *Forum Equorum* in the reign of Edward I) and White Lion Street (saddlers). The Maddermarket has already been mentioned and to this can perhaps be added Wensum Street (*Vicus Cocorum* or Cookrow).

The Market Place itself, originally laid out in the eleventh century, had the greatest range of goods for sale. Poultry, sheep, cattle, wheat, wood and cheese were sold to the south of St Peter Mancroft church. To the north were drapers, linen drapers, clothiers, glovers, spicers, ironmongers, shoemakers, butchers, fishermen, cutlers, hatters and goldsmiths. There was even an apothecary market (*Forum Unguentor*). Tolls and customs were collected in the Murage Loft.

The survival of works of art implies that the city acted as a centre for specialized activities. It is likely that the writing and decoration of books was practised in Norwich and the Ormesby Psalter, now in the Bodleian Library, Oxford, is probably an example of such local output. Decorative ironworking, some of which survives on the doors of the cathedral infirmary from as early as 1180, was also a local craft, with further examples on the doors of the Carnary College at the cathedral dating from about 1316–37.

Sculpture must have been practised in Norwich. The large-scale sculpture of the medieval city has all been destroyed (the last example, probably a Christ in Majesty from the Ethelbert Gate, as late as 1964) but the wealth of small sculpture, particularly in the bosses at the cathedral or the south chapel of St Helen, and on the exquisite Prior's Door of about 1310, suggests a significant school. A stone carver called 'Guillaume de Nourriche' worked in Paris between 1297 and 1330 and may have been an expatriate product of such a school; an apostle by him is in the Musée de Cluny.

Population and housing

The range of goods and services available in Norwich implies a large population, a conclusion endorsed by the apparent continued growth in the number of churches. Excluding religious houses, nearly 60 parish churches are known to have existed in the thirteenth century, with very few going out of use. St Christopher seems to have burnt down before 1286 and was not rebuilt; St Edward was united with St Julian before 1300; and St John the Evangelist was pulled down about 1300. Development for insurance offices on the site of St John in 1964 removed much of the graveyard of this church.

This large number of churches, assuming a minimum congregation of some 250 souls to a church, implies a population of at least 15,000 people in the city. Recent analysis of the Mancroft Tithing Roll, however, would suggest that this could be a considerable underestimate. Extrapolation from the Mancroft sample indicates that a more realistic assessment would be a population well in excess of 20,000 and possibly as high as 30,000. Such numbers in the Middle Ages implied a great city indeed and it is small wonder that Norwich was a complex organization, tied together by its bridges and churches and surrounded by its extensive city wall.

Excavation is beginning to provide considerable information on the lives of this medieval population. Housing, for example, is an area where little survives above ground to indicate the conditions within which people existed. It is becoming clear that the majority of people in the thirteenth and early fourteenth centuries

49 *Wooden roofing shingle with iron fastening discovered at St Martin-at-Palace Plain in 1981 (*Steven Ashley*).*

occupied either timber-built structures or buildings with clay walls. These houses were usually single storeyed and frequently had only one room. A central hearth was often, but not always, provided.

Examples of clay-walled buildings have been located at Alms Lane, Bishopgate, Botolph Street and, outside the city wall, on Heigham Street. Documentary evidence mentions such structures as in 1287, when Richard, son of William Pikot, and Matilda his wife granted a piece of land in Lower Newport (St Giles Street) to John le Lung, chaplain, and undertook 'that a wall of earth shall be built at the joint expense of the parties'. Occasionally there is evidence of clay and stone being used together, as at Westwick Street where excavation in 1972 demonstrated that the long walls of a building were supported by stone but the gable walls were of clay. Thatch was probably the most common roofing material but the recovery of an oak shingle at St Martin-at-Palace Plain in 1981 (complete with iron nail for attachment) demonstrated that wooden tiles were used too (**49**).

Post-built or clay buildings seem therefore to have been the norm for the mass of the population. Excavation also has the greatest potential as the primary source for information about buildings of greater social status at this period. No building belonging to the merchant class survives from the thirteenth century, although it can be surmised that many such structures would have been built with rubble ground-floor walls and timber-framing above (as was probably the case on the site of Dragon Hall, King Street).

The large population of Norwich was thus probably housed in generally poor conditions. The numbers of people would also have produced great quantities of rubbish material. Much of this was inevitably disposed of in rear tenement yards, with some night soil presumably manuring the fields around the city. There seems also to have been a trade in muck; the Great Plumstead estate paid for muck to be brought from Norwich in both 1277–8 and 1298–9. The trade was probably long lasting, as the muck boat was repaired in 1319–20.

It would appear that significant quantities of rubbish were also dumped at the river margins, not only to level up wharfage sites but also to remove lowlying land from danger of inundation. This would explain, for instance, the extensive deposits of rubbish material, mixed with occasional flood deposits, located off Whitefriars on the north bank of the river. Floods were a considerable problem in the thirteenth-century city. A particularly bad flood, recorded in 1290 by Bartholomew Cotton, 'overturned some houses and bore them along'. A freshwater flood deposit was discovered within the stone building excavated at Palace Plain in 1981. Attempts were made to prevent flood incursions; the threshold of the north doorway of the stone building, which fronted the river, was raised and the lower part of the doorway blocked by inserted flintwork.

The increasing numbers of people in the thirteenth century, and thus of houses, meant that much of the tenement pattern of the medieval city was established at this time, with boundaries either being created afresh or being established through subdivision of existing plots. Excavations on Westwick Street have demonstrated that twelfth-century boundaries lasted into the twentieth century, and the same phenomenon has now been observed on the north bank of the river at Calvert Street. Here a boundary between two properties was marked initially by a wooden fence, the large post-holes for which were clearly visible. These respected the position of the now anachronistic Anglo-Scandinavian defensive bank, implying that the boundary was established by the twelfth century at the latest. It was succeeded by a flint wall with this, in turn, being replaced by a brick wall and the boundary again surviving until recent times.

This development of the urban geographic pattern was one which also removed existing streets where these were no longer used to great effect. In 1250 Roger de Burg was fined for obstructing the King's way upon the quay (at the eastern end of Quayside) and was ordered to clear his purpresture or encroachment. He may have done so but in 1285–6 four further defendants – including Maud de Catton (mentioned above, p. 66) – were all accused of blocking the quay and of having 'built Houses there to the nuisance of ye whole City & of all Passengers and Boats there arriving...'. These houses may have remained, despite orders for their demolition, for the line of Quayside is blocked on the earliest detailed map of the city (1558) and remains blocked to this day.

The people who lived and died in the city were generally buried in the local cemeteries around the parish churches. While some 30 parish churches survive, another 30 or so have been lost (many in the sixteenth century). It is inevitable that redevelopment will affect such sites on occasion, and graveyard assemblages (as well as church sites) were destroyed at St John the Evangelist, St Martin-in-Balliva and St Botolph in 1962, 1970 and 1974 respectively.

The assemblage at St Margaret *in Combusto* was excavated, however, partly in 1973 and extensively in 1987.

It was observed above (p.60) that this grave-yard came into use about 1100. It developed a particular function, however, as the suffix to the church dedication makes clear: St Margaret *ubi sepeliuntur suspensi* ('where those who have been hanged are buried'). The common gallows stood outside the Magdalen Gate, the church-yard being only some 100m (330ft) inside the city wall, and it seems very probable that numbers of the skeletons recovered were those of executed criminals.

The normal pattern for Christian burial is for the body to be interred supine (that is, on the back) with the head to the west and the

50 *Seven burials interred top-to-toe in a single grave-cut, St Margaret* in Combusto, *1987 (*Kirk Laws-Chapman*)*.

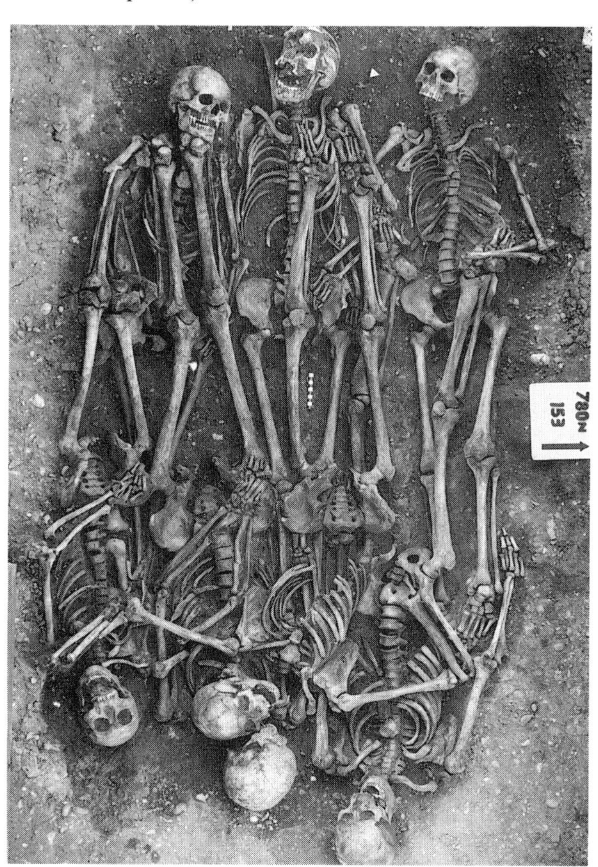

feet to the east. This was the predominant pattern at the graveyard of St Margaret but some burials were interred in a reversed fashion – east to west; others were buried prone (that is, face down); some were buried north to south; and some had clearly been thrown into pits with little ceremony. Quite frequently individuals in pits or prone had their hands behind their backs, implying that they were tied.

It seems likely that many of these were criminals who had been hanged. Occasionally skeletons were located where it was clear that the body was fully clothed at burial. Buckles and fragments of cloth with eyelets for lacing survived. Bodies tended to be stripped for burial and these clothed individuals could therefore be execution victims. It is also possible, however, that some at least were the victims of plague or epidemic. There were a number of group burials which might imply as much, including one group where seven individuals were interred in a single pit, laid out top-to-toe alternately (**50**). A further group of individuals was interred with the arms of the bodies around each other. Most burials remained discrete but this was a poor parish, probably the poorest in the city, and no individual could afford an expensive imported stone coffin. At least one, however, was buried within a grave which had been lined with flint and mortar to give the impression of a freestone coffin.

This skeletal assemblage is very important because it is a large group from a relatively short-use cemetery (it went out of use by the end of the fifteenth century) and it contains individuals who died in the prime of life, either from execution or disease. It will thus provide extraordinarily useful data as the material is analysed. Preliminary results are encouraging: for instance, at least one individual appears to have suffered from syphilis, evidence that the disease was present in Europe prior to Columbus' discovery of America.

It is also encouraging to note, however, that at least one man may have got away. In 1345 Henry, son of John le Satere, was hanged for felony. Thomas Davy, a clerk, cut him down and took him to St Margaret for burial 'as is the custom'. Before he could be buried, however, Henry revived – presumably Davy had cut him down too soon. Davy was imprisoned for his pains although the further fate of Henry remains unknown.

The later castle

Henry may well have been tried at the Shirehall as he was hanged at the castle, which is where the Shirehall was situated. The earliest record of the *Curia Comitatus* is in 1287 and it stood on Castle Hill, probably within the south bailey. It was built of stone and was in ruins by the reign of Elizabeth. There is a suggestion that it stood on its own low mound, which perhaps explains why no trace of it was found in recent extensive excavations. Landscaping in the eighteenth and nineteenth centuries would have removed the mound and with it any residual elements of the building.

The landscaping could not, however, eradicate the massive defensive improvements to the castle which were undertaken in the early

51 *Excavation of the barbican ditch in 1990: a collapsed part of the barbican gateway lies in the upper fills to the top right of the photograph (*Kirk Laws-Chapman*).*

thirteenth century. Possibly inspired by the fall of the castle to Prince Louis, Dauphin of France, in 1216 (it was taken without a siege), it was refortified by the construction of a ditch some 12m (39ft) deep and 20m (60ft) wide across the south bailey in front of the mound (**51**). On the inside of this barbican ditch, a large defensive gateway was constructed of flint with limestone dressings, probably as an extension of the gate towers at the foot of the mound bridge (**52**). Probably demolished between the sixteenth and eighteenth centuries, substantial fragments of masonry survived in the upper fills of the ditch, one containing recesses for the hinge supports of a great door, another traces of a window or doorway.

The plan of the gateway could not be recovered, as all foundations and foundation trenches were destroyed by the cutting of a road in 1862. A large well, 3m (10ft) square and 42m (135ft) deep, was discovered, however, and excavated to a depth of 25m (81ft). This probably provided a defended water supply within the gatehouse. The rubble fill contained

53 *Vault beneath the Bigod Tower, Norwich Castle. It is scorched, possibly as a result of incursion in 1174 or 1216 (*copyright, World Art Studies, University of East Anglia*).*

objects such as a limestone block carved for a game of nine men's morris, the bridge of a musical instrument, a limestone mould for the manufacture of copper alloy belt chapes and two gilded mounts decorated with spread eagles. The gateway may have been complicated, controlling access to the south and also to the west, where it can be suggested that there may have been a gate to the French borough, linking the castle directly with the Jewry and the market place.

The castle remained a royal fortification but it was an increasingly anachronistic institution. It may have been besieged in 1174, when the city was attacked by the Flemings, as well as in 1216 (either of these events could have been responsible for the scorching of the elaborate early Norman vault which survives as a support for part of the now-lost Bigod Tower adjacent to the keep, **53**) but, by the early fourteenth century, the defences were in considerable disrepair and some citizens were encroaching upon the Castle Fee.

As an example, William Bateman, who held property on Timberhill in 1304, was prosecuted for extending his tenement into the King's land. The results of excavation in 1989 are still being assessed, but it is possible that tenement boundaries of properties on Timberhill were extended at this time across the line of the probable Fee ditch, encroaching on Crown land. The castle keep was already being used

52 *Recording the remains of the barbican gateway in 1990; this fragment lies on its side following demolition, possibly in 1738 (*Kirk Laws-Chapman*).*

as a gaol in the fourteenth century and, in 1345, the castle area was transferred to the city (except for the mound and the south gate) in the second charter of Edward III.

The city maintained the castle 'ditches', as the area was called, as open space, licensing the grazing of animals. There were a number of other such areas within the walled circuit. To the north was Gildencroft (p. 66); much of the area around the church of St Margaret *in Combusto* was almost certainly open land; the cathedral close encompassed much open space, while the Prior's Fee also included *Cowholme*, summer pasture next to the river; tenting grounds for stretching cloth lay in St Giles parish; Newgate or Surrey Street was probably only built up as far as All Saints' Green and thereafter was open land; and the Butter Hills, inside the southern defences, were also open space.

The Friars

Some of this open land began to be colonized by religious institutions in the thirteenth century. The first friars, Franciscans, arrived in the city in 1226. They occupied a large site to the east of the castle, on land which had been occupied in the Saxo-Norman period but had either been depopulated in the aftermath of the Conquest or was cleared for the friary. A church, that of St John the Evangelist, was taken over by the friars and closed, the parish being added to that of St Peter Parmentergate about 1300. The site of the precinct extended towards the river to the east and was served by a stream, the Dallingfleet. This was crossed by a stone bridge which survived until as late as 1888 and may still survive beneath the modern roadway (**54**).

Nothing remains of the friary above ground but excavations in 1992–93 revealed that substantial structures and deposits survive below ground. The site was markedly steeper than is indicated by present day topography with noticeable changes in level. The church buildings seem to have stood where the upper end of Prince of Wales Road (an 1860s' street) stands, but south of this were cloisters and

54 *Drawing of the stone bridge on the Horsefair published in 1888. This bridge was part of the Franciscan Friary and crossed the Dallingfleet stream or cockey; it may still stand below ground (*Norfolk and Norwich Archaeological Society*).*

claustral buildings. Excavations uncovered footings of these together with vaulted culverts (**55**), probably for the friary water supply although possibly acting as drains. A substantial flint wall, almost 2m (6ft) high and over 60m (195ft) long, ran west to east, apparently

55 *Culverts excavated on the site of the Franciscan Friary in 1993. They formed a complex system, possibly channelling water from a spring on King Street to the west (*Sarah Reilly*).*

56 *Boundary wall of flint, probably between claustral buildings and allotments or orchards, excavated at the Franciscan Friary in 1993 (*David Wicks*).*

dividing the buildings from the gardens, orchards and allotments on the southern perimeter of the precinct (**56**).

The Dominicans also arrived in 1226 and settled north of the river off Colegate. Their site embraced the church of St John the Baptist, which was closed and amalgamated with St George Colegate in the thirteenth century. After 1307, however, the Dominicans acquired a more central site south of the river, although the Colegate site was retained and used again in the fifteenth century. Nothing now remains north of the river above ground but substantial later medieval structures survive on the post-1307 site, the most complete friary complex in the country.

This survival, predominantly of fifteenth-century structures (p. 89), is due to the city purchasing the precinct in 1540. In so doing, the city also acquired the friary archives, including the deeds of properties which went to make up the precinct. It is thus possible to reconstruct the process whereby the Dominicans acquired land and to determine the approximate layout of pre-friary topography.

Tenement histories of late thirteenth- and early fourteenth-century date can be compiled, with the last owner before the friars frequently being a man called William But. It is difficult to escape the conclusion that he was acting as an agent for the friars, acquiring property on their behalf as they were not supposed to engage in property transactions. The abuttals on many of the deeds allow the tenements to be grouped geographically so that an idea of the urban complexity of the area can be established.

Despite the fact that the Dominicans were establishing a precinct on such an urban area, the northern part of their site was marginal land, lowlying and adjacent to the river. Excavations in the cloister, which lay to the north of the church, in 1974 and again in 1992, have revealed the massive dumping of rubbish material which was necessary in order to raise the land here to allow building.

The Carmelites or White Friars established their friary in 1256. It too was built on marginal land and stood next to the river, north of Whitefriars Bridge. As with most of the other precincts, the site is largely destroyed above ground although an arch survives at the entrance to the printing works which now occupies the area. A vaulted undercroft also still stands, the walls of which date to the fourteenth century. Foundations of the church were observed in 1904 and skeletons were found during building works in the 1950s and 1960s (including a rare late fourteenth-century rectangular oak coffin now preserved in the St Peter Hungate Church Museum in Norwich). The only modern controlled excavation was undertaken in 1976 within the undercroft. This located traces of pre-friary deposits, including a timber-framed but clay-walled building.

The most extraordinary survival from the friary itself, however, is no longer on the site. This is an early fourteenth-century arch of limestone with vine leaf decoration, carved dragons and other beasts, the head of a bearded man at the apex, and flanking female figures and kings set within smaller arched niches.

Although known to have been set within a porch at Arminghall Old Hall, south of Norwich, from the sixteenth century until 1910, the arch was almost certainly removed from the friary at the time of the Reformation. It has now been returned to Norwich and re-erected inside the Magistrates' Courts, on the south bank of the river opposite the site of the friary. The original function of this arch is difficult to determine, but it has been argued that it formed a gateway or a porch.

The fourth great friary was that of the Austin Friars. They settled in Norwich in 1290 on a large site next to the Wensum off King Street. They too took over the site of a church (St Michael Conesford) and closed it about 1360. Little or nothing remains of the precinct. The site was subjected to massive development in 1970 with only minimal recording possible by two undergraduates from the University of East Anglia. The site was sloping, which enhanced the preservation of buried walls, and these were found standing in excess of 2m ($6^1/_2$ft) in height across the site. They were all swept away.

Other friars also settled in Norwich. The Sack Friars were established about 1254 but their order was suppressed in 1307 and their site passed to the Dominicans. The Pied Friars were also suppressed in 1307 and their house, to the north of the churchyard of St Peter Parmentergate, became a college of priests. Elements of buildings, including an arcade, appear to survive within later structures. Friars of Our Lady seem to have lived south of the church of St Julian and, for a while, Carmelites were established within a house in the churchyard of St Martin in Balliva, close to the Castle.

Hospitals and colleges

The establishment of friaries was augmented by the establishment of further hospitals. The greatest of these was the Hospital of St Giles or the Great Hospital on Bishopgate, founded in 1249 by Walter Suffield, Bishop of Norwich, for 'poor and decrepit' chaplains and thirteen other poor people. Much of the institution survives, with the infirmary hall, refectory and screens passage, as well as a beautiful fifteenth-century cloister. Hildebrond's Hospital, a common hall for poor people established by Hildebrond and his wife Maud in 1216, stood in the southern ward of Conesford. This foundation was subsequently attached to the church of St Edward but nothing now remains of either.

While there were numerous other small ecclesiastical foundations throughout the city, the other great thirteenth-century establishment was that of the College of St Mary in the Fields. This was founded about 1250 and stood in the western part of the city, close to the churches of St Peter Mancroft and St Stephen. It functioned as a community of priests and had its own church with a cloister and claustral buildings. Although largely destroyed at the Reformation, elements of it survive within the fabric of the later Assembly House (including an undercroft) and the broad plan of the establishment is known. Recently, refurbishment work at the adjacent Theatre Royal necessitated the demolition of a wall within which was located a carved label stop depicting a bishop. This fourteenth-century carving was almost certainly from the college and may represent a benefactor (**57**).

The growth of institutions in the thirteenth century was not entirely ecclesiastical, although the foundation of a school north of the Close and next to the river owed its origin to monks of the Cathedral priory. The site of this school is cleared and awaiting redevelopment; it is hoped that excavation will be possible in the near future. A toll-house was also established in the thirteenth century (by 1290 at the latest). It stood on the site of the existing Guildhall and, as well as being used to collect tolls, it also acted as a law court and prison.

It would be a mistake, however, to view the history of Norwich in the thirteenth and early fourteenth centuries as one of unalloyed growth and success. There were setbacks, some considerable. It has already been noted that the castle fell to the Dauphin of France in 1216. In 1266 rebellious barons called 'The Disinherited' raided Norwich and reputedly carried off a hundred and forty carts of loot. The most far-reaching incident was probably the riot of 1272 when the citizens, apparently under extreme provocation from the prior, attacked the cathedral precinct, burning down the Ethelbert Gate and St Ethelbert's church, sacking the cloisters and also burning much of the cathedral church. The king himself came to Norwich to restore order. The effects of the fire can still be seen on the Ethelbert Gate and in parts of the cathedral, while St Ethelbert's church was never rebuilt and the remains lie buried under the lawn of Almary Green. The stone building excavated at St Martin-at-Palace Plain was apparently destroyed at about this time; as it was a cathedral property outside the protection of the precinct, it may have been one of the first to suffer in the riot. It would remain a ruin for over a hundred years.

Despite such events, Norwich by the 1340s was a greatly enhanced city with a burgeoning population, increasing wealth and major secular and ecclesiastical institutions. It had weathered setbacks to emerge as the dominant city of East Anglia with a commercial network which embraced local, regional, national and international trade. Disaster, however, was lying in wait.

57 *Label stop of fourteenth-century date depicting a bishop, recovered during building works at the Theatre Royal in early 1992. Probably from the College of St Mary-in-the-Fields* (Steven Ashley).

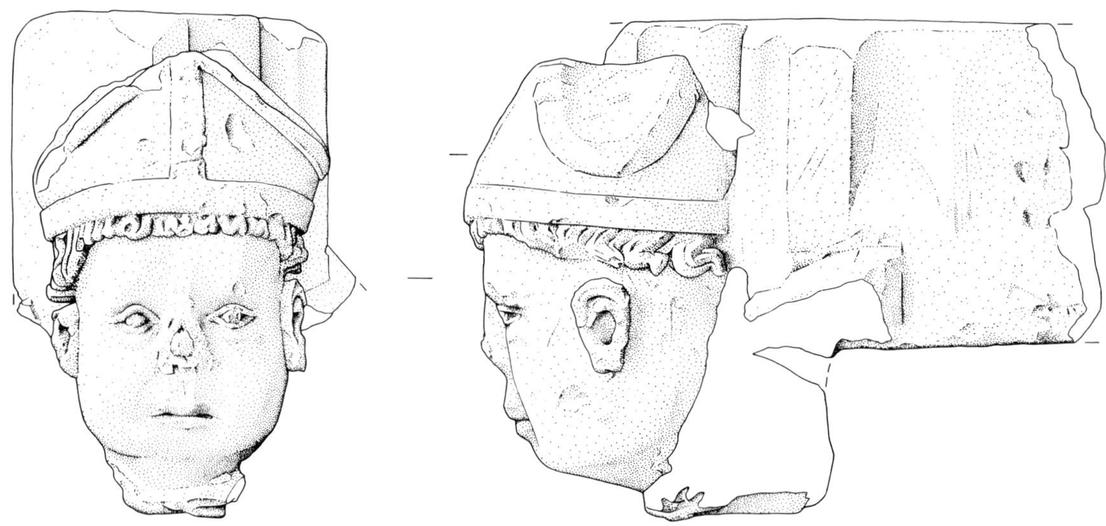

6

From Black Death to Great Fire

About 1377 the parish of St Mathew, a small church immediately outside the north wall of the Cathedral Close, was added to that of St Martin-at-Palace. It had suffered grievously at the time of the Black Death in 1349 and had never recovered. In this it was not alone; the parish of St Catherine or St Winwaloy in the southern part of the city seems to have become completely depopulated; St Anne on King Street was added to St Clement Conesford about 1370; and depopulation seems to have led to the disuse of St Margaret Newbridge, where the chancel came to serve as a hermitage for a hermit charged with looking after the bridge.

It is probable that pestilence claimed as many as one in three of the population, consistent with evidence from elsewhere in the country. In the short term the effect upon the economy of the city must have been intense although this is difficult to assess in the material evidence which survives, other than in losses of marginal churches such as St Catherine or St Margaret. The church at New Bridge was almost certainly one of the latest to be founded in Norwich, on reclaimed land next to the Wensum. Its endowment must have been small and it was therefore vulnerable at times of stress.

The city seems, nevertheless, to have recovered rapidly. Interestingly, although there were further church losses in the fifteenth century (usually as a result of amalgamation of parishes), generally the number remained static. Indeed, by the late fourteenth century, the evidence of the surviving churches seems to indicate a renewal of investment rather than retrenchment. Building additions, in the form either of added aisles or chantries, became common throughout the city, paving the way for massive rebuilding campaigns of certain churches in the fifteenth century. As examples, the chancel of St Gregory was rebuilt in 1394 and the aisles of St Martin-at-Palace date from the late fourteenth century, as does the lower section of the tower of St Stephen.

St Gregory's chancel was built at the expense of the cathedral priory but much other investment in churches seem to have been the result of private benefaction. Many older merchant families disappear from records at the time of the Black Death, but late fourteenth-century Norwich was still a city which contained wealthy individuals and these did not hesitate to display their wealth at home as well as at church, producing monuments which still stand.

The urban élite

As early as 1370, the father of William Appleyard, the first mayor of Norwich, probably built the house now known as the Bridewell. It occupies a block of property between two streets, with the house itself set back from the street frontages. The building, one of the eighteen late medieval secular houses to survive in Norwich, was constructed on a grand scale with a suite of vaulted undercrofts beneath its

58 *The knapped and squared flint north wall of William Appleyard's house, first Mayor of Norwich (now the Bridewell Museum). This is almost certainly the wall which Celia Fiennes was taken to see in 1698* (Brian Ayers).

northern and eastern ranges. The public face of the north range is a *tour de force* of squared and knapped flint, most probably the wall seen by Celia Fiennes in 1698 (p. 10) (**58**).

Other such houses include Strangers' Hall (now a museum, like the Bridewell). This began as a fourteenth-century hall at right-angles to the street, above an early brick-vaulted undercroft with stone ribs. It was rebuilt in courtyard style in the fifteenth century with the hall parallel to the street although retaining the undercroft. Quoins of the fourteenth-century building can be seen in the courtyard, as can quoins of a further building in the yard of the Plough Inn on St Benedict's Street. Elsewhere, excavations uncovered the footings of a fourteenth-century house of more modest pretensions at St Martin-at-Palace Plain (supplementing records made in 1962 when it was demolished).

These are all grand structures of an affluent elite, many of whose members operated as an oligarchy controlling the city. In many ways the development of the power of this oligarchy defined the development of the city as a distinct institution. Recognition of the oligarchy's power and importance came in 1404, when the city acquired the right to self-government through a mayor and aldermen. This was, however, more of a formalization of a growing sense of corporate identity which can be traced back to at least the thirteenth century. Corporate ownership and responsibility for property, for instance, dated from at least 1250, as the construction of communal defences illustrates. Acquisition of the Castle Fee and extension of city control over waste land in 1345 extended holdings and, after the Black Death, the wealth of the late fourteenth-century city was also to be made manifest in public buildings and corporate control.

Initially such increases to the corporate portfolio were acquisitions. The city bought up shops and market stalls and controlled the sale of meat, poultry and fish. In 1379 the Old and New Common Staithes were acquired on King Street in order to control goods and shipping. Nothing remains of either above ground, but the site of the New Common Staith is cleared for development and may reveal evidence for both medieval wharfage structures and trade (the City made a contract with one John Marwe in 1432 to replace the old wooden staith with a new one of stone).

In 1384 the city acquired a large site north of the market place to act as a cloth seld, or public hall for the sealing and control of cloth (it also acted as a hostel for foreign merchants). It is likely that large parts of this building (or a sixteenth-century successor) survived until 1963, when it was pulled down without record (it is thought that the range on the Pottergate frontage was 31ft (9.5m) wide). Much of the area is, nevertheless, still a rabbit warren of structures, many of which could contain elements of this important structure.

At the end of the fourteenth century, the city undertook the first of several major building initiatives. A tower known as the *donjon* or Dungeon Tower, in the angle of the river Wensum, had been acquired from the Great Hospital in 1378 (although the documentary evidence is less than clear cut). A remarkable document in the Treasurer's Roll of 1398–99, however, indicates that the tower was completely rebuilt at this date, producing the structure which stands to the present day, known as the Cow Tower (**59**).

The building was surveyed in 1985–86 and is interpreted as a freestanding artillery tower, with gun emplacements on the roof and loops for hand guns within embrasures on the first and second floors. It was furnished with latrines and hearths and, probably, a vaulted undercroft. Faced in brick (almost all of which survives), the core of the fabric contains large quantities of flint. It provided defence for the city at a vulnerable spot where the river is overlooked by the high ground of Mousehold Heath, and was connected to the fortified Bishop Bridge (to the south) and the city (to the east) by a palisade which ran along the river bank.

The Treasurer's Roll is valuable not only for

59 *Part of the Chamberlains' Account for 1398–99 detailing payment to workers and for materials at the Cow Tower (*Norfolk and Norwich Record Office/Norfolk Museums Service).

dating the construction of the Cow Tower but also for the detail it provides concerning the processes involved and materials needed. It lists the workmen, the days worked and payments made for miscellaneous items. Carters, carpenters, masons and labourers all worked on the tower, while payments were also made to stone-miners who must have supplied the flint. Bricks were bought from a variety of sources and small items were also recorded: 1d for the carriage of a *cabyll*; 10d for the hire of a boat at various times to carry *hirdeles*; 2d for a *Wyndynhook* for the windlass; 6d for a *barell*; 6d to make four *tubbes* from the said *barell*; and 19d for 'payments for drink at various times'. The total account, which was rendered in Latin with the exception of occasional words in English as italicized here, was £36 17s 2½d.

The Cow Tower was clearly a major undertaking and is unique in that such a comprehensive documentary account survives for a building so little altered. The city oligarchy was soon involved in further considerable expenditure. A new guildhall was erected on the site of the old tollhouse between 1407 and 1412. Designed as one of the most splendid of provincial guildhalls, this also still stands (although drastically 'restored' in the 1860s) with a fine example of East Anglian flint diaper work on the exterior east façade.

Other early fifteenth-century expenditure included a new Market Cross in 1411 (this was replaced in 1501–03) and construction of city water mills at New Mills. These were completed in 1410 but problems with the sluices led to serious flooding in the suburb of Heigham upstream, and the mills were not effectively operational until 1430. They defined the head of the Wensum as they straddled the river; the site is now occupied by a fine nineteenth-century pumping station.

The corporate body of the city was therefore a major element in Norwich society by the beginning of the fifteenth century. The city was able to act increasingly as an independent institution (although riots in the 1430s and

1440s twice led to brief seizure by the King). This independence may have assisted the more affluent against the less wealthy. It is clear from various documentary sources that the oligarchy was not universally popular. In addition, given that in the fifteenth century the wealth of the city overall seems to have been in decline, the fact that many of the major surviving medieval structures were built or rebuilt at this time emphasizes that the greater merchant class still had disposable income, presumably at the expense of their neighbours.

Buildings

The buildings which resulted from the disposal of this income were both domestic and ecclesiastic. Few of the former survive, although examples do exist and are occasionally recognized afresh. One such is the Old Barge or Dragon Hall on King Street, effectively rediscovered after 1979 with the gradual removal of later partitions. Here, an existing building seems to have been bought by one Robert Toppes in the 1430s, partly demolished and rebuilt as an enlarged, grand new structure. This consisted of an inserted brick-vaulted

60 *Carved openwork spandrel depicting a dragon in Dragon Hall, King Street. Elements of the original paint survive (*Kirk Laws-Chapman*).*

undercroft, reuse of a hall range at right-angles to the street and the construction of a massive timber-framed first floor hall parallel to and running the length of the street frontage.

This hall is surmounted by a crown-post roof with a spandrel between the tiebeam and a brace containing an openwork painted carving of a dragon (**60**) (hence the modern name of the building; there is evidence that other spandrels also contained carvings). The front elevation is slightly jettied, with a surviving decorated corbel at the southern end. At the rear of the building is an arcade which extends from the screens passage associated with the earlier hall wing. The rear arcade includes a large timber arch facing the river with, inside it, a similar brick arch in the ground-floor rubble wall of the building.

This major fifteenth-century rebuilding must have been associated with river traffic and trade and, indeed, Toppes is known to have been an affluent cloth merchant with extensive landholdings in north Norfolk. The first-floor hall was divided into two parts and it is thought that the northern end, served by the arches, would have acted as a display and selling area for cloth, with the more private southern end being used for business transactions and domestic matters.

Dragon Hall is not the only building on King Street to have been refurbished in the fifteenth century. The Music House, the twelfth-century hall of the Jews Jurnet and Isaac, also had a brick-vaulted undercroft inserted within the street range south of Jurnet's hall. The building was refurbished upstairs too, including the insertion of a scissor-brace roof. This probably came from demolition of a wider building elsewhere; the prefabrication numbering system on the timber was ignored, the roof being inserted to fit the existing walls with earlier mortice joints for ashlar pieces in the underside of the rafters remaining unused.

At St Martin-at-Palace Plain, the twelfth-century stone building, which was probably demolished in the late thirteenth century

(p. 76), was brought back into use by the creation of a vault of brick above three inserted piers of brick and flint. The vault had to be 'crippled' around existing apertures and corbels survived in the walls to show where ribs to effect this crippling had run. This new vault supported a rebuilt structure above, probably a timber-framed building, glimpses of which can be seen behind a Georgian facade in photographs of the 1940s. It was demolished by 1956.

Other fifteenth-century houses were new-built. Among these are the west range of Bacon House on the corner of St George's Street and Colegate; the street range of the building recently discovered and restored on Fye Bridge Street and now known as The King Of Hearts; and Suckling House on St Andrew's Street. This building has a high crown-post and scissor-brace roof with a brick bay window (reconstructed in the twentieth century) facing into a small courtyard. Its nearest parallel is Stranger's Hall, itself rebuilt in the fifteenth century incorporating earlier elements, where a similar bay window, albeit in stone, survives.

Windows were clearly important features of the houses of the affluent at this time. A fourteenth-century house at Palace Plain had a bay window added in the fifteenth century (it was demolished in 1962 but re-erected nearby in 1970) and a similar bay window partly survives at the Great Hall, Oak Street (**61**). Slightly later, in the sixteenth century, large windows were used in the rear range of The King of Hearts and also in the rear range of the Plough Inn on St Benedict's Street.

Fireplaces were also grand in the greater houses: side columns of a fifteenth-century example were recovered from St Mary's Plain in 1959. Wall paintings are also known: fragments of a painting depicting a knight in armour on horseback survive from the demolished White Swan Inn. Buildings were sometimes adorned with carved wooden brackets as with the figure of a young man, also from the White Swan (**62**) (one of several – the others disappeared at the time of demolition), or the

61 *Arch to the bay window in the Great Hall, Oak Street. The building was an open hall but a floor was inserted subsequently, dividing the arch. Similar examples are known from St Martin-at-Palace Plain (demolished 1962) and Pykerell's House, St Mary's Plain (Kirk Laws-Chapman).*

sixteenth-century example still in place on Garsett House, St Andrew's Hall Plain.

These buildings are all exceptional structures in that, firstly, they survive and that, secondly, they represent the most affluent level in medieval society. As such they are atypical, but all domestic buildings of less affluent groups have disappeared (even Pykerell's House on St Mary's Plain, one of the smallest surviving fifteenth-century buildings, is a house of quality). It is only possible to recover the plan and history of the vast remainder through excavation. This was done most effectively at Pottergate in 1974 for houses of intermediate status and at Alms Lane in 1976 for poorer structures.

The site at the corner of Pottergate and St Laurence's Lane was devastated by fire on 25 March 1507. A building range of late fifteenth-century date on the Pottergate frontage, probably divided into three houses, was destroyed and not rebuilt until the seventeenth century. Each house had a cellar roofed in timber and the collapse of the building range also entailed

62 *Carved figure of* c. *1400 recovered from the White Swan Inn during demolition in 1962. The figure is attached to a bracket (above) which was in turn tenoned to the building* (Karen Guffogg).

the collapse of much of the contents of the houses into the cellars. Excavation therefore recovered not only evidence of the structures but also a dated collection of contents, helping to determine the social status of the occupants.

It is clear that the buildings did not house the urban poor. The cellar walls were of flint with brick quoins. Lamp niches and windows were also fashioned in brick. The windows would have been in the north wall where the land fell away; here too was a stair to the ground floor, also of brick with treads of quartered tree trunks. Cesspits provided sanitation, one at least being fed by a chute. It is probable that each of the three buildings was gable-end on to the street and of two storeys. Each probably had timber-framed party walls with ground floor walls of flint rubble and brick and was heated, perhaps by stoves, as fragments of stove-tile were recovered, the earliest evidence in England for the use of closed stoves. The easternmost house may have had hearths of plain and glazed Flemish floor tiles.

The contents of the cellars were particularly rich in kitchen equipment and included cooking pots, a skillet (**63**), fragments of a colander, a

63 *Copper alloy skillet from a building on the corner of Pottergate and St Laurence Lane destroyed by fire in 1507* (Norwich Survey).

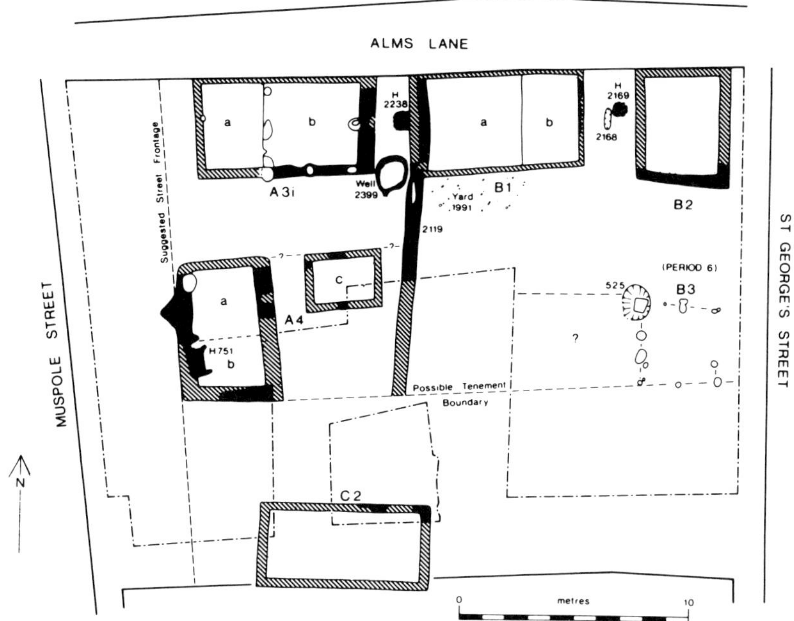

64 *Plan of houses at Alms Lane, St George's Street and Muspole Street in the fifteenth century (*Norwich Survey*).*

long-handled cooking pan, a skimmer, a strike-a-light and part of a spit. Other finds included candlesticks, painted glass, horticultural implements, a terracotta plaque which possibly depicts St John the Baptist, and door furniture. The buildings were small in scale but well built and their contents suggest that the occupants were comparatively affluent. The discoveries seem to demonstrate the sort of structure that reasonably prosperous citizens could expect to inhabit in the late fifteenth century without the ostentation of the great courtyard houses of the truly wealthy.

Excavations at Alms Lane in 1976 uncovered evidence for more modest dwellings (**64**). Here, buildings of the first half of the fifteenth century were constructed with clay walls, occasionally interspersed with timber posts, were of one storey and of two rooms. In only one building was there any trace of heating by a hearth.

These structures largely continued in use during the second half of the century, clay again being used for walls although the addition of timbers in one structure is interpreted as being to allow the construction of a loft. Floors were generally of clay and may have been covered with rush matting. Heating was becoming more common with hearths being constructed next to walls and furnished with a simple chimney or a hood. Rubbish disposal seems to have been rudimentary; only one cesspit was located and this was a clay-lined pit rather than a stone construction as at Pottergate.

The vast majority of the population would have occupied buildings similar to those at Alms Lane. Although such structures could exist side by side with more affluent buildings (the fifteenth-century west wing of Bacon House stands across the road from the Alms Lane site), most of the better houses were in the richest parishes of the heart of the city, those of SS Andrew, Giles, Peter Mancroft and Stephen.

Undercrofts

This much can be gleaned from the documentation (all the goldsmiths in fourteenth-century Norwich lived in the parish of St Peter Mancroft for example) but more material evidence is available in the structures of the city. While

65 *Part of the vaulted undercroft at Strangers' Hall* (Kirk Laws-Chapman).

nearly all the medieval secular buildings have been lost, undercrofts built beneath them by the merchant class frequently survive (**65**). These structures, built of flint and brick and, by virtue of their design, wholly or partly buried, often escaped fires and demolition intact and were reused in later buildings. Many that were not so reused are discovered by excavation (usually although not always without their vaults) or were bricked up and survive sealed.

Over 60 such undercrofts, almost all of them of fifteenth-century date, are known to exist within Norwich and the sites of 34 others are known. Most are on the south bank of the river Wensum, exploiting hillside sites in, generally, the four most affluent parishes of the city. They were frequently built into the hill, providing a flat platform for house construction above but with ground-floor access to the cellar at the lower part of the slope.

Most of the undercrofts have rectangular plans with walls of flint. The roofs can be groined or barrel-vaulted with the provision of ribs, wall arches, axial piers and side chambers as necessary. Ribs and webbing are of brick with little variation in rib form. Lamp niches are usually located in the walls, fashioned in brick and frequently opposite the entrance. Many undercrofts can be accessed from within the building, usually by a stair of brick although this is not always the case; some could only be entered by external doors, normally from the side or rear of the property.

The single largest suite of undercrofts is that below the Bridewell Museum which dates in part to the late fourteenth century (**66**). The complex plan ultimately comprised an L-shaped undercroft which began with ten compartments of vaulting arranged around three central piers and two bays around a central lateral rib. Two separate additions extended the suite to the west with octopartite vaulting. Deviations in the rib patterns indicate missing doorways and windows (the undercrofts are only partly below ground). Detailed study of the structures has enabled sequences of alteration to the building above to be postulated.

The Bridewell was a grand house but the intensive use of space by undercrofts is found elsewhere such as beneath No. 4 Tombland, where there is a three-bayed undercroft with six side chambers, single-chamfered diagonal ribs, lateral ribs and wall arches. A further structure of two bays and an end chamber on Redwell Street is linked by a vaulted side passage, with stairs leading from this passage to a side entrance.

Undercrofts (**67**) are not only extant within secular structures. Probably the finest architectural example within the city is that located within the Dominican Friary complex (and now known as The Crypt – it is used as a cafe). The brick walls probably date from 1258–67, a very early use of brick as a building material, but the vault was added in the fifteenth century. Although restored, it is a high ribbed vault dividing the square crypt into four bays. An undercroft also survives at the site of the Carmelite Friary off Whitefriars. The walls here are predominantly fourteenth-century in date (with fifteenth-century extensions) but the vault was again added in the fifteenth century. Piers of brick were constructed to allow springing of the ribs.

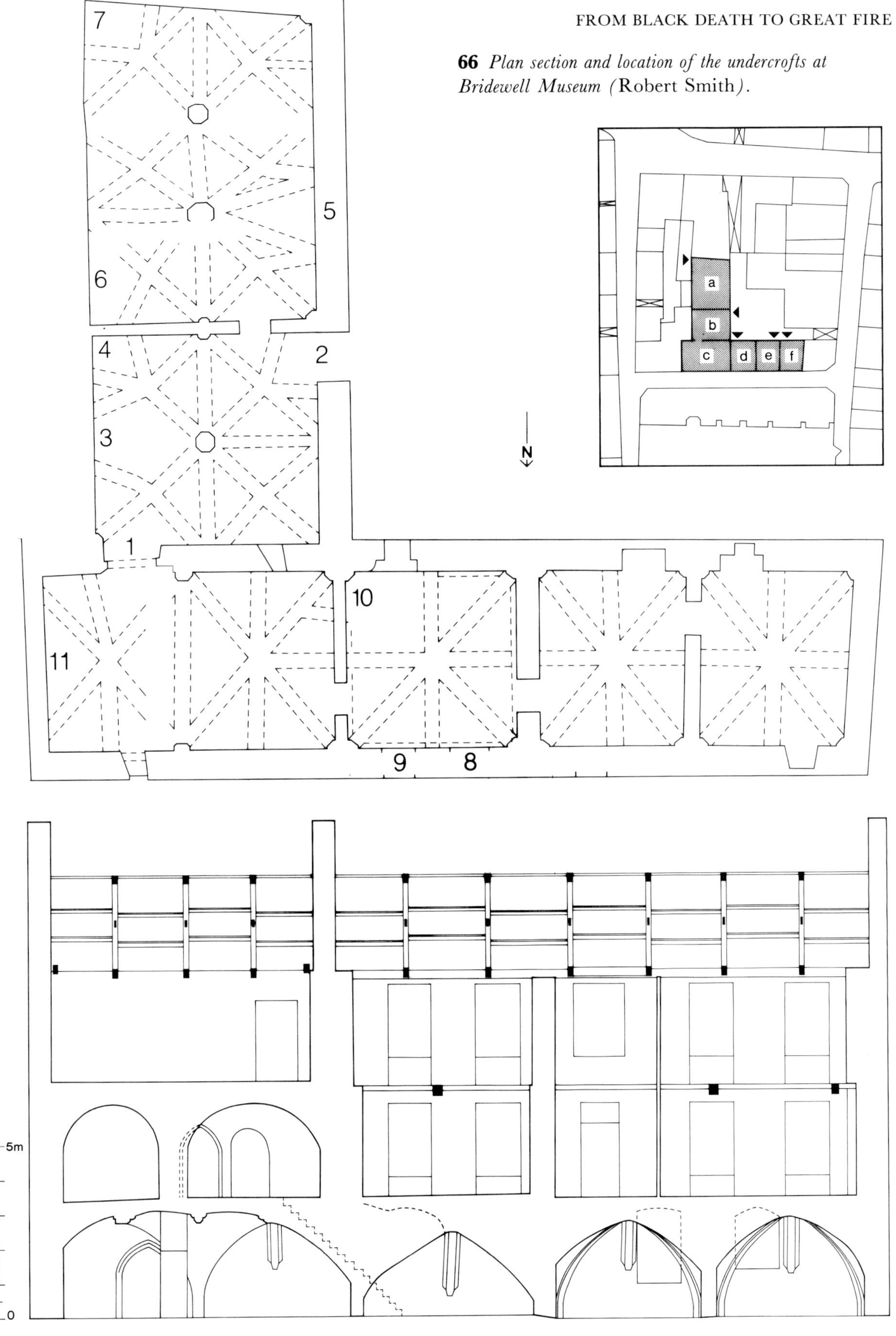

66 *Plan section and location of the undercrofts at Bridewell Museum (*Robert Smith*).*

Building materials

The increasingly widespread use of brick in the fifteenth century can be noted throughout the city. The spire of the cathedral was rebuilt about 1480 by Bishop Goldwell after an earlier one had fallen in a storm in 1362; it is of brick encased in stone. Similarly, the piers at the church of St Swithin are rendered and lime-washed to give the appearance of stone but are, again, of brick. Stairs in numerous buildings, particularly church porches and as access to towers and rood lofts, are of brick and drains and conduits were increasingly lined and vaulted with brick. Detailing was increasingly undertaken in brick; refurbishment of the excavated stone building at Palace Plain necessitated the use of chamfered brick for the window dressings to replace robbed earlier dressings of Barnack limestone.

Brick manufacture may have taken place immediately outside the western wall of the city, as there were brickfields here in the post-medieval period. Much brick could have been imported, probably by water from the eastern part of the county. A last of 'Tyle' (probably 'wall tile', meaning brick) was purchased from St Benet's Abbey on the River Bure in 1388–89 where it is likely that there were brick kilns and tileries. Importation of brick has a long history in Norwich; large bricks were purchased from Flanders in the 1260s to provide a curtain wall around the top of the mound at the castle.

While bricks, and of course tiles, were needed for building campaigns in the fifteenth century, a greater need was for stone and lime. The houses of the richer merchants used large quantities of flint and mortar but these were still relatively minor amounts compared to those required for major ecclesiastical rebuilding programmes. The church of St Peter Mancroft, the most splendid parish church in Norwich, was entirely rebuilt in the years 1430–55; the Dominican Friary was largely destroyed by fire in 1413 and was eventually completed in 1470; the church of St Andrew seems to have been rebuilt completely between 1450 and 1520; and

St George Colegate was rebuilt from about 1459 to 1513.

Flint and lime were available in quantity locally and were quarried both within and outside the city walls. A large part of the Ber Street escarpment in the southern area of the walled city, between Ber Street and King Street, was exploited in this way and the steep wooded slopes which still survive here are the remains of a relict industrial landscape. The provision of freestone to Norwich was more difficult, the nearest decent freestone coming from Northamptonshire quarries. The greater churches were not thwarted, however; Mancroft obtained stone from Ancaster and was left 40s in 1506 to pave the chancel in marble; the cathedral, for which stone had been brought from Caen in the late eleventh and twelfth centuries, was buying stone in Purbeck, Dublin and Clipsham in the fourteenth century; and recent excavations at the Franciscan Friary have identified Purbeck marble in floorings of probable fifteenth-century date.

Sand and gravel were also quarried. Quantities of these materials were extracted on Mousehold Heath, where an early map depicts 'ston mynes', but there is also increasing evidence for such quarrying from excavation sites in the city centre. Relatively extensive extraction, for example, was being undertaken within the Castle precinct before the end of the Middle Ages. This extraction was particularly great against the disused south-western rampart of the south bailey, so much so that the rampart had to be cut back in the fifteenth century and revetted with a stone wall.

The workmen and craftsmen who effected the late fourteenth- and fifteenth-century rebuilding of Norwich remain largely anonymous, although some are known through sources such as the Cow Tower account (a number of labourers are mentioned by name here) or because of their skills. Two masons, Robert Everard and John Antell, occupied adjoining houses at Palace Plain in 1483. Everard worked at the cathedral (he provided the nave vault

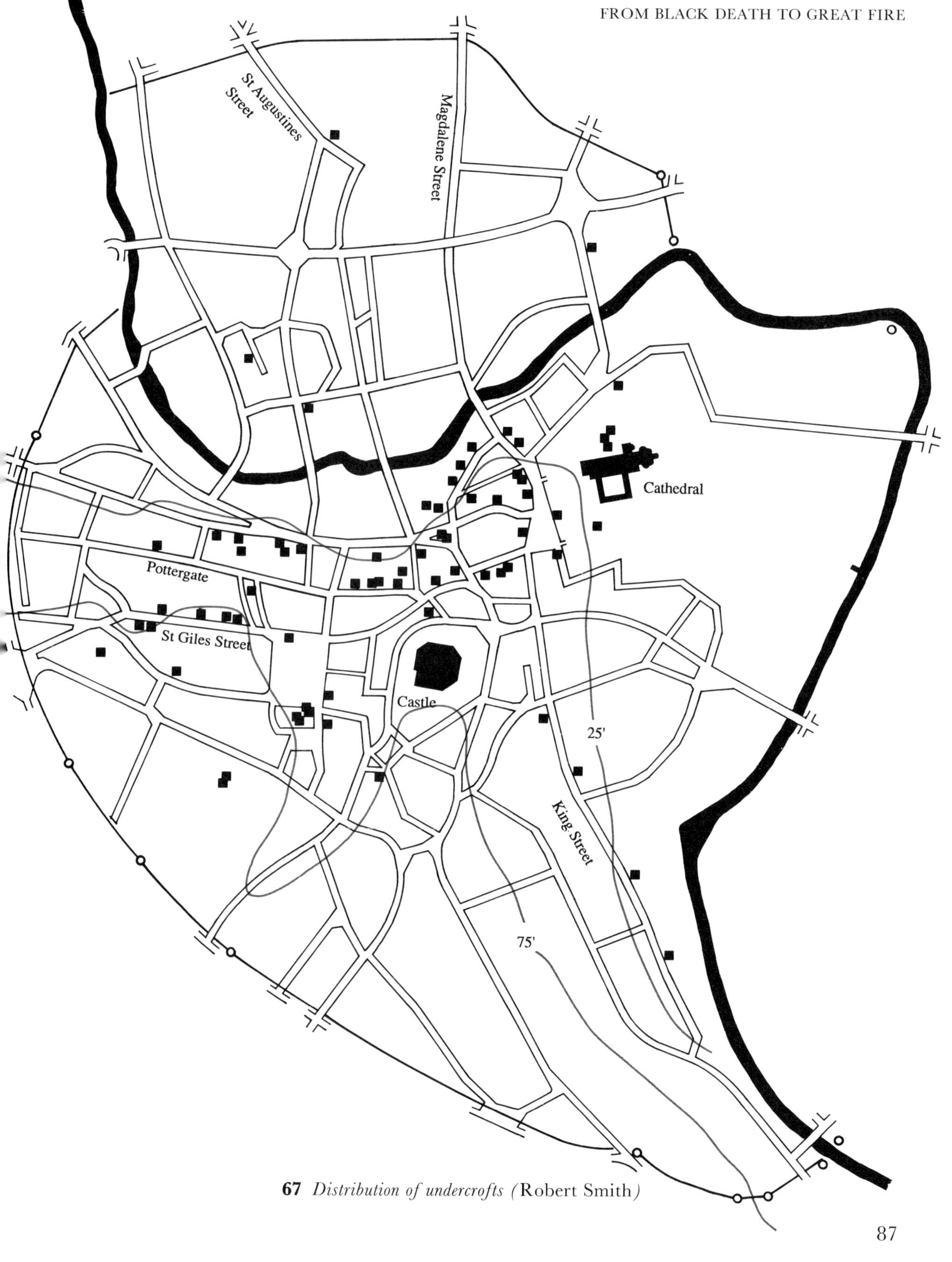

67 *Distribution of undercrofts (Robert Smith)*

for Bishop Walter Lyhart) and Antell has been recognized as the mason responsible for work at the churches of St George Colegate, St Martin-at-Oak and St Michael Coslany. He seems to have had a workshop on Bishopgate. Evidence for a masons' yard was recently excavated at the cathedral, where a deposit of limestone dust and chippings was discovered in an enclosed area north of the nave.

The churches

Although archaeological excavation has been helping to clarify the development of secular buildings in late medieval Norwich, results to date on church excavations have been limited. Only one standing church has been submitted to a reasonably thorough excavation – that of St Martin-at-Palace in 1988 – and even here work was largely confined to the nave. Nevertheless, it was possible to establish a sequence of development, despite floor deposits being severely damaged by post-medieval intrusive burial (**68**).

More limited work at the church of St James in 1979 was also able to examine a sequence of construction including major rebuilding in the fifteenth century. Excavation in 1972 on the

68 *Excavation within the church of St Martin-at-Palace 1987 showing post-pits of earlier structures and the striped foundation of the Saxo-Norman church (*Martin Smith*).*

site of the bombed church of St Benedict recovered a sequence of ground plans and, together with documentation and architectural detailing which was either recorded before or survived the bombing, was able to establish that fifteenth-century alterations included the addition of western and eastern bays, a chapel and a porch to the north aisle and the insertion of a clerestory. The site of the church at St Margaret *in Combusto* had been completely destroyed by cellars and thus was not excavated when its graveyard was uncovered in 1987; a fragment of window tracery was recovered, however, from the remains of an adjacent sixteenth-century cellar.

Archaeological examination of the growth of churches may be limited (although details of ecclesiastical life have been recovered, such as a fourteenth-century pewter chalice and paten from the grave of a priest at Carrow Priory) but considerable information can be gleaned from later medieval wills for works which were effected in churches. At St Laurence, for instance, bequests were made for work on the tower in 1468, 1470, 1472, 1473, 1479 and, finally, in 1508 'to fynyshyng of ye stepyll'. In St George Tombland bequests for the roof were made in 1447 and 1518; one such repair may have led to the curious loss of a piece of fifteenth-century chain mail discovered in the roof of the south aisle in 1963. One of the most famous examples of benefaction was at the church of St Peter Hungate, where the roof was paid for by Margaret and John Paston; label stops in the south transept may represent them.

Expansion of churches occasionally caused problems within the cramped topography of the medieval city centre. Applications were made on occasion to close lanes, as was done successfully for the Dominican Friary in 1345. More frequently, churches were built across thoroughfares as at St John Maddermarket where a passageway pierces the tower or St Gregory where the chancel is built above a lane. A similar situation probably prevailed at the east end of St Peter Mancroft; although here the lane was eventually pushed further east and the archway beneath the chancel incorporated as part of a 'processional way' (an undercroft survives below the existing Weavers Lane, immediately east of St Peter Mancoft, perhaps implying a lost building above).

The continual burial of individuals within churchyards led to problems of overspill. The phenomenon, and its topographical effect, was noted by John Evelyn in 1671:

> One thing I observ'd of remarkable in this Citty, that most of the Church-yards (though some of them large enough) were filled up with earth, or rather the congestion of dead bodies on(e) upon another, for want of Earth &c to the very top of the Walls, & many above the wales, so as the Churches seem'd to be built in pitts....

In theory, overspill could be accommodated from the early fourteenth century by the charnel house established at the cathedral (the Carnary College, now part of the Norwich School). In practice, other solutions were found. Excavation in 1988 beneath the car park of the Maid's Head Hotel off Palace Street located graves associated with a lost burial chapel. This graveyard and chapel had acted as overspill for the churchyard of SS Simon and Jude since at least 1316 although they were located within the parish of St George Tombland. It may have been disused by the early fifteenth century.

Churches did not just expand or were rebuilt in the fifteenth century; some continued to be lost, such as that of St Margaret *in Combusto*. This was added to All Saints Fyebridgegate about 1468; St Clement Conesford was added to St Julian in 1482; and St Cuthbert may have disappeared before 1492. Elements of St Cuthbert's church, including the south wall of the nave (or south aisle), were observed in the 1930s during construction of an office building and skeletons were recorded in 1952 when these were disturbed by drainage work. Further skeletons were recorded on the site of the graveyard of St Clement Conesford in 1962

during bulldozing. The church of St Clement itself survived into the eighteenth century, reused as a barn.

Encroachment upon graveyards was not unknown. The eastern graveyard of the church of St George Tombland was probably cut back in the later Middle Ages, as a revival of commercial activity on Tombland led to the establishment of small shops without rear yards on the street frontage (the establishment of St George, probably in the twelfth century, had itself encroached upon Tombland).

Churches could also be associated with industrial activity. A bellfounding pit, together with numbers of bell mould fragments, was excavated to the north of the church of St John the Baptist Timberhill in 1989, within the graveyard. The Timberhill area housed a number of bellfounders in the fifteenth century whose products were marketed throughout Norfolk.

The great ecclesiastical institutions founded in earlier centuries continued to thrive. The predominantly fifteenth-century building campaign at the Dominican Friary can be followed in the buildings themselves as purchase of the complex by the city in 1540 has ensured much of their survival. The large preaching nave still stands; with simple piers devoid of ostentatious decoration and an equally simple but soaring hammerbeam roof. The east end of the nave would have been walled off from a central walking space. This wall no longer exists but its footings were observed and recorded during flooring repairs in 1993. East of the walking space is the choir with a great decorated east window.

Considerations of space on a marginal riverine site dictated that the cloisters were constructed to the north. The south walk of these is intact, with elements of the east and west walks also surviving. The plan of the north walk has been recovered by excavation (**69**), which has also uncovered part of the chapter house, pier shafts of which survive, and the brewhouse.

South of the church was a preaching yard, still an open space. The friars were anxious to

69 *Excavation of the Dominican cloisters in 1910/11*
*(*Norfolk and Norwich Archaeological Society*).*

preach to the population and a yard surface uncovered on excavations at the Franciscan Friary probably indicates the location of another such yard. The Dominicans also owned all the property in the angle south-east of the church, formed by the corner of Elm Hill and Princes Street. Buildings here are post-medieval in all but one or two have medieval cellars, one with a lamp niche, implying that there may have been friary structures here too.

The friary provided a cell for an anchorite, remains of which stand adjacent to the exterior north wall of the choir with a squint through the wall to the high altar. There were a number of anchorages in Norwich, the most famous being that attached to the church of St Julian and occupied in the early fifteenth century by the celebrated mystic, Julian of Norwich. The city seems also to have been host to two or three beguinages, women living as religious communities but without vows. One such community may have been housed in the Britons Arms, a fifteenth-century thatched building on Elm Hill.

Trade and industry

Norwich in the fifteenth century continued to be a major industrial city. Much of this industrial output was directed at the textile trade, although this seems to have suffered a decline relative to its fourteenth-century peak. Dyers and other cloth-finishers nevertheless continued to operate. Excavation on the north side of Westwick Street at the foot of Letestere Row in 1972 uncovered a fifteenth-century dyer's workshop. Here a late thirteenth- or early fourteenth-century building had been adapted for dying with the provision of furnaces, a stoke pit, well and drain. The building remained in use into the sixteenth century.

Artefacts provide further evidence of the textile trade. Wool combs dating from the twelfth to seventeenth centuries have been recovered. Tenter hooks are also known, used when dyed cloth was stretched on tenting frames; the earliest example is fifteenth-century in date. An iron harbick, used to secure cloth to the cropping board during shearing, was found at a site on Oak Street.

Fullers, tanners and skinners all continued to exploit their river frontage sites in the fifteenth century as their predecessors had done earlier in the Middle Ages. Other industries were also important. 'Dornix', a type of cloth used for wall hangings and bed coverings, was supplementing worsted as an important product. The city was also developing its specialized industries, Norwich painted glass being particularly important in the fifteenth century. Great quantities of this were smashed in the seventeenth century but good examples still survive, notably in the east window of the church of St Peter Mancroft and in the Guildhall. It is likely that the production of works of art to adorn churches and the houses of the merchant class was also undertaken in Norwich; the Despencer retable at the cathedral is almost certainly of local craftsmanship.

Commercially the market suffered in the aftermath of the plague but recovered in the late fourteenth century. Finds of pottery and other artefacts testify to the city's trade contacts in the later Middle Ages. As examples, two complete Spanish vessels together with fifteenth-century Italian majolica were found at All Saints Green in 1970. The commercial

90

importance of the river continued to be recognized, although many goods were shipped by barge from Great Yarmouth where most maritime trade was now centred. The construction of Dragon Hall, almost certainly to facilitate the sale of cloth, took place at the waterfront where transhipment was easiest. The provision of a covered passageway beneath the wide rear arcade at Dragon Hall parallels the covered arcades of warehouses at King's Lynn and other ports, enabling goods to be sheltered quickly.

Clerics as well as merchants sought such frontages; the Abbot of Wendling in central Norfolk had a staith at Abbey Lane which he leased to the city but where he maintained a brewery, presumably using water from the river. Other houses with a riverside location included Binham, Bromholm, Chicksand, Ely, Hickling, Sawterie (Sawtry, Hampshire) and Woburn.

The existence of such buildings emphasizes the importance of Norwich as both an administrative and trading centre. At least 42 ecclesiastical institutions had houses in Norwich to administer their trade and provide hostels for their staff. The Cistercian monasteries of Vaudey (Lincolnshire), Pipewell (Northamptonshire), Merivale and Combe (Warwickshire), Warden (Bedfordshire) and Garendon (Leicestershire) all had property in the city. Traces of such buildings occasionally survive or are recovered by excavation. Elements of the city house of the Priory of Augustinian Canons at Ixworth in Suffolk still stand on Colegate. The Abbot of Waltham maintained a property on Fishergate, part of which was excavated in 1985. The city house of the Abbey of North Creake (near Burnham Market in north-west Norfolk) was excavated in 1978 on the corner of St Martin's Lane and Oak Street.

This excavation was the most comprehensive to date on such a building of a religious institution in Norwich. The abbey seems to have acquired the property and built a house about 1332. Creake was a poor foundation and the first building was a mean two-roomed structure of clay walls, although with two hearths, set back from the Oak Street frontage. This was rebuilt as a two-roomed range up to the frontage in the fifteenth century with brick and flint rubble walls and a range of three rooms behind it. Two of these rooms were clay-walled, implying that they were single storey in contrast to the street frontage range. Two ovens in one of the rooms suggests that it was a kitchen or bakehouse.

The rural gentry also owned property in the city. The Paston family are the most famous examples, owning houses on Elm Hill and King Street, but other famous names included those of Heydon, Berney, Coke and Hobart. Sir Thomas Erpingham had a large house off World's End Lane at the beginning of the fifteenth century. Substantial parts of this survived until 1858, when it was demolished to make way for a gasworks. Its construction had entailed encroachment upon the river by some 25ft and it was furnished with a tower. Destruction by the gasworks was thorough, however, and nothing remained for archaeological recording when the site was observed during a watching brief in 1985.

Norwich at the end of the fifteenth century was therefore an affluent city with major secular and ecclesiastical buildings and institutions, a diverse economic base and a regional importance. The evidence for its material culture comes from both surviving buildings and, increasingly, from archaeological excavations. The size and diversity of property throughout the city, and the evidence for the social organization and economic commitment needed to enable Norwich to function effectively, illustrate a city able to adapt to both political and pandemic disaster. The sixteenth century was to bring even greater change, starting with two further disasters in one year, the *annus horribilis* of 1507.

7

The post-medieval city

At the beginning of the sixteenth century, the Almoner of Norwich Cathedral Priory was in difficulty with his accounts. Rents, formerly £10 a year, had fallen to only 19s 4d. The reasons given for this were 'the great fires', the evidence for which was summarized by Blomefield in the eighteenth century: 'on the 25th day of April [modern scholarship has redated this to March] 1507 a fire broke out, which burnt with continual violence four days...', followed in June the same year by 'another lamentable fire, which burnt two days and a night'. Blomefield calculated that some 718 houses with most of their goods were burnt in 16 parishes (**70**).

The fires were clearly devastating and affected some of the most affluent as well as impoverished parts of the city. They were not the sole reason for the almoner's difficulties, however; rents had been declining for some years but the drop in 1507 was certainly dramatic. The disaster, therefore, added to the economic problems of early sixteenth-century Norwich but was not the cause of them.

It is unclear how the city responded to this crisis, other than by a measure enacted in 1509 to ensure that buildings were to be covered in tile rather than reed. Probably some forty per cent of the housing stock had been destroyed, inevitably placing considerable pressure on the surviving structures. Archaeological evidence, particularly from the 1976 excavations at Alms Lane, suggests that, while there was some new building with flint and brick walled structures, in general the exploitation of the existing site was intensified with the infilling of yards and the expansion of existing buildings.

This evidence complements work elsewhere

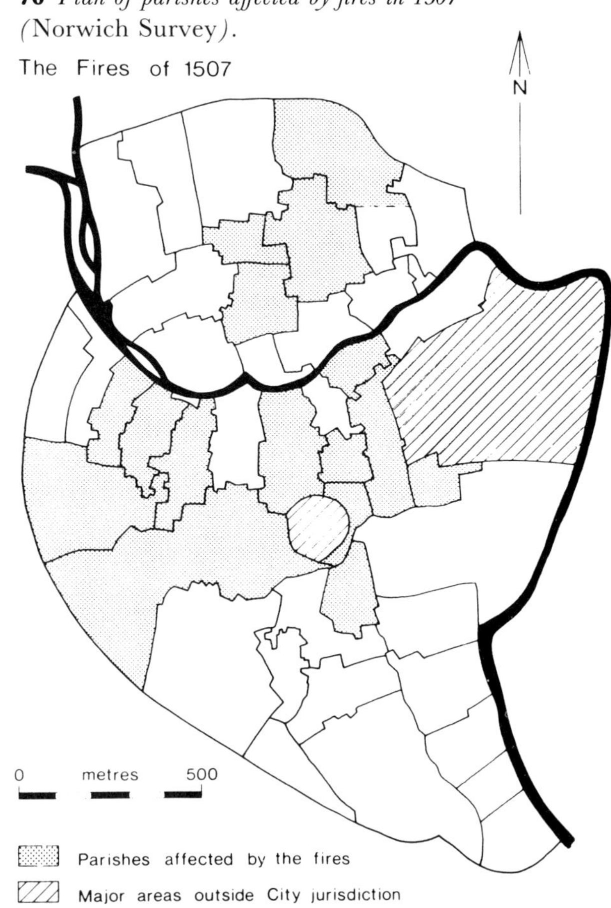

70 *Plan of parishes affected by fires in 1507 (Norwich Survey).*

which indicates that not all the sites devastated by fire were rebuilt immediately. Buildings destroyed on the corner of Pottergate and St Laurence's Lane were not replaced until the seventeenth century. This was not atypical; the City considered the situation so bad in 1534 that it sought to compel rebuilding or enclosure of land with a wall. As late as 1570 the City Assembly could record that, resulting from fire, 'many goodly buyldinges and howses are becom gardens and orteyards wheare somtyme enhabited artificers and others...'.

It has been suggested, nevertheless, that the 'great rebuilding', noted elsewhere in later sixteenth-century England, may have begun a generation or more earlier in Norwich, in part due to the perforce circumstances induced by the fires. There is some cartographic evidence to support this idea; the 'Sanctuary Plan' of 1541 is the earliest-known map of the city and, although crude, illustrates some seventy or so houses. Nearly all of these have a chimney, implying a degree of sophistication across the city, perhaps inspired by fire-control measures introduced following the 1507 disaster.

It therefore remains difficult to clarify the situation concerning the housing stock of the early sixteenth century. Further excavation will help, as will examination of surviving buildings. Although only some 214 buildings predating 1700 are known to survive, it is likely that about 200 of these date to the sixteenth and seventeenth centuries. It is probable that different development chronologies will be discovered for different parts of the city, reflecting social and economic factors as much as recovery from fire devastation.

Recovery was not helped by a general economic malaise in the city at the beginning of the sixteenth century. Worsted exports in particular were suffering and protectionist legislation and regulation did little to revive this moribund industry. The malaise dragged on into the mid century; weeds were growing in the market place in 1544 and, in the previous year, a herd of cows interrupted a service in the neighbouring

71 *Bacon House, Colegate showing the western end of the sixteenth-century range with the tower of St George beyond (*Brian Ayers*).*

church of St Peter Mancroft.

There was, nevertheless, still wealth in Norwich and ostentatious displays to indicate this survive. The great of the city were still building, either houses, as at Bacon House on Colegate (**71**) where the spectacular street frontage dates in part from the 1530s, or in donations to churches – the Thorpe chapel of St Michael Coslany was constructed about 1500 with an impressive display of flushwork decoration. The wealthy merchant Robert Jannys had a terracotta tomb made for the church of St George Colegate (either by the same craftsman who made the famous Bedingfeld tombs at Oxborough or using the same moulds) while, slightly more modestly, Philip Curson left money in 1506 to pave the chancel of St Peter Mancroft in marble.

The ostentation spilt over into public buildings. A market cross some 60–70ft (20m) high, standing on a plinth 30ft (9m) wide, was built at the expense of John Rightwise in 1501–03 (it was demolished in 1732 and the footings were probably those uncovered in 1909 and described as 'massive remains') while a grand Council Chamber was erected in 1535. These were the endowments of rich men who helped to make Norwich the highest taxed provincial city in the 1520s, but whose expenditure and public profile masked a much larger underclass of urban poor and relatively impoverished artisans.

The Reformation

The Reformation necessarily brought considerable disruption to the city. Much of Norwich and its surrounding area was dominated by the great monastic institutions, notably those of the Cathedral Priory and the Priory of Carrow. Large parts of the city were given over to monastic precincts and there were numerous hospitals, chantries, anchorages and a school. Removal of these in the 1530s and 1540s severely disrupted the local economy but also released much land for development.

An example of rapid exploitation of the new circumstances is that undertaken by Thomas Howard, the third duke of Norfolk. He was granted 'the site, church, house, bells, fisheries, yards, buildings and all possessions' of the Franciscan Friary in Norwich in 1539. While he did not immediately clear the site (the 'great house' of the Friary, probably the living quarters of the friars, was pulled down in 1565–66 at the charge of the city), he certainly began to ransack the structures. Repairs about 1540 to the Blackfriars were assisted by '17 loads of paving tile brought from the Greyfriars' while a new buttery and pantry were built 'with spars of the Grey Friars chancel roof'.

Demolition of the Franciscan Friary was thorough. Excavations on the site in 1993 found few walls surviving above foundation level and nearly all freestone gone. Great dumps of waste material consisted entirely of mortar and small fragments of flint; all other material had been removed. Floor tiles had been lifted (possibly for the repairs at the Blackfriars) and marble was also taken although two marble floor slabs were overlooked and survived to be recorded.

Other sites were probably also cleared. A ruined wall and arch are depicted on Cuningham's plan of 1558 on the site of the Carmelite Friary but the church had gone. The site of the Norman hospital is shown as open space although buildings are known to have been standing in 1571. The Augustinian Friary was demolished and eventually became a celebrated garden. The old Blackfriars site off Colegate was open land in 1558.

Some monastic structures were reused, those of the Dominicans being the most outstanding examples (p.89). The Carnary College was acquired for use as a grammar school (replacing the dissolved monastic school), thus ensuring its survival. The Great Hospital was refounded with a new constitution, so it too survived. A further outstanding survival is that of the early sixteenth-century Prioress's wing at Carrow. This was built by Isabelle Wygun (her rebus of the letter 'y' with a cannon or gun is extant in a spandrel of a doorway in the west wall) and was converted in the eighteenth century into a house. It now forms part of the staff facilities for Colman's factory.

Churches were also lost or went out of use at or shortly after the time of the Reformation. Losses were the churches of All Saints, Fyebridgegate which was gone by 1551; St Bartholomew on Ber Street (by 1550; see **72**); St Botolph (by 1548); St Crowche (by 1551); St Martin in Balliva (about 1558); St Mary in the Marsh (about 1564); St Mary Unbrent (about 1540); and St Olave (1546). The church of St Mary the Less was added to St George Tombland in 1542 but the building still stands.

With minor exceptions, there is no surviving visible evidence of the lost churches. Elements of some of them continue, nevertheless, to influence the modern urban topography or

72 *Interior of St Bartholomew's Church, Ber Street, disused since the sixteenth century, in 1931. The building was destroyed during the Second World War (*Norfolk and Norwich Archaeological Society*).*

exist within later structures. It seems likely that All Saints was sold, the nave passing to one purchaser and the chancel to another. The site of the nave is now occupied by a Co-op store on Magdalen Street while that of the chancel is waste ground. St Bartholomew was still standing in the 1930s when its interior was photographed in use as a store (**72**); it was bombed in the Second World War and only one corner of the west end now survives.

The site of St Botolph was destroyed without record for the Anglia Square development in 1974 but anonymous information recounts the numerous skeletons uncovered at the time. The site of St Martin in Balliva was also destroyed with little record in 1970, although skeletons were found together with quantities of pins, perhaps implying burial in shrouds. Parts of the church and graveyard may yet survive and a stone coffin, uncovered in road works in 1910, was probably from the site.

The city was the centre of activity during Kett's Rebellion of 1549 when it was besieged by an army of rebels estimated at 30,000. The rebels established headquarters buildings on the edge of Mousehold Heath in the recently-dissolved St Leonard's Priory and St Michael's Chapel (the remains of the latter are still known as 'Kett's Castle'). The attack on the city led to partial destruction of the Cow Tower where the battlements were hit by cannon fire. The rebels took the city from the east but were in turn forced out by royal forces under the Earl of Warwick. He breached the western walls and other damage included the firing of houses, the demolition of Whitefriars Bridge and burning of buildings at the Common Staith and the Great Hospital. Traces of burning still exist at the top of the Cow Tower.

While Norwich thus had both economic and political problems during the first half of the sixteenth century, it remained nevertheless a city of the first rank. It had achieved this without any major contribution by the noblest families of the land and, indeed, directly royal and aristocratic influence in Norwich is notable for its absence through much of the later medieval period.

Attempts to obtain such influence were made in the sixteenth century. The Earl of Surrey built a house on Surrey Street before 1513 (it survived into the nineteenth century) with a successor earl eventually acquiring the site of the Augustinian Friary and erecting a fine seventeenth-century house there. The Duke of Norfolk, however, determined to build a palace in Norwich and this was erected between 1561 and 1567. The site chosen was hardly propitious; anxious to be close to the centre of a populous city, the Duke acquired the only place available, next to the river downstream of the dyers. A visitor in 1681 (shortly after refurbishment of the building) described it as a 'sumptuous new-built house, not yet finished within, but seated in a dung-hole place ...'. It was never a popular residence.

Excavations in 1974 (the palace was abandoned before 1711 and most buildings destroyed by 1806, although the bowling alley survived into the twentieth century and was photographed) revealed that enormous quantities of soil had been brought in to level up the site prior to building. Massive brick foundations were inserted but none of these reached bedrock (the infill overlies a gravel terrace) and cracking occurred in the walls. A staircase tower, probably part of the kitchens, and outbuildings were discovered. There was considerable evidence of the reuse of materials, probably from ecclesiastical sites in the city, but also from further afield; a memorial slab was found on the site in 1849 from the Abbey of St Benet at Holme, east of Norwich on the river Bure.

The 'Strangers'

The Duke of Norfolk was not the only 'incomer' (a Norfolk term) to the city in the sixteenth century. In 1565, the city authorities invited 'Dutch' cloth manufacturers to settle in the city. Initially the invitation extended to 24 Dutch and six Walloon master weavers but

73 *Sixteenth-century shop front on Bedford Street, the earliest to survive in Norwich. It originally formed part of a row of shops* (Brian Ayers).

numbers increased rapidly so that by 1579 there were about 6000 'Strangers' in the city. Plague in that year killed disproportionately large numbers of these immigrants, probably as a result of cramped living conditions, but by the early seventeenth century it is probable that they constituted one third of the population.

The social impact must have been great (and occasional movements to expel them are known) but their economic importance was even greater. The Strangers effectively revitalized the stagnant Norwich cloth trade, introducing new techniques and fabrics and laying the basis for the extraordinary wealth of the city in the seventeenth and early eighteenth centuries.

The Strangers left their mark on the city. The church of St Mary the Less, 'the French church', probably survives because it was used by the Walloons. The choir of the Dominican Friary, now known as Blackfriars Hall, was the Dutch church and an annual service in Dutch continued to be held until early in the present century. A great number of the Strangers settled initially on the north bank of the river Wensum, in parishes such as that of St George Colegate. Documentary research has uncovered surnames of individuals and family groups such as Ceuleman, De Clerke, Dierick, Fromanteels, Moenes and Vancuelen.

Excavations on the north bank, both at Alms Lane in 1976 and, a little further to the north, at Calvert Street in 1989–90, recovered evidence of probable Dutch communities. Finds included dress fittings, hair ornaments and clay pipes of Dutch type or manufacture. An eighteenth-century structure at Alms Lane, with a base for a copper, was interpreted as a wash-house, perhaps for scouring yarn. A Walloon weaver, Jacob Votier, was a tenant on the site in 1725. Low Countries pottery was common from both excavations although this need not necessarily reflect Dutch occupation; many sites in Norwich contain fragments of such vessels which were clearly in widespread use from the later medieval period. Some vessel

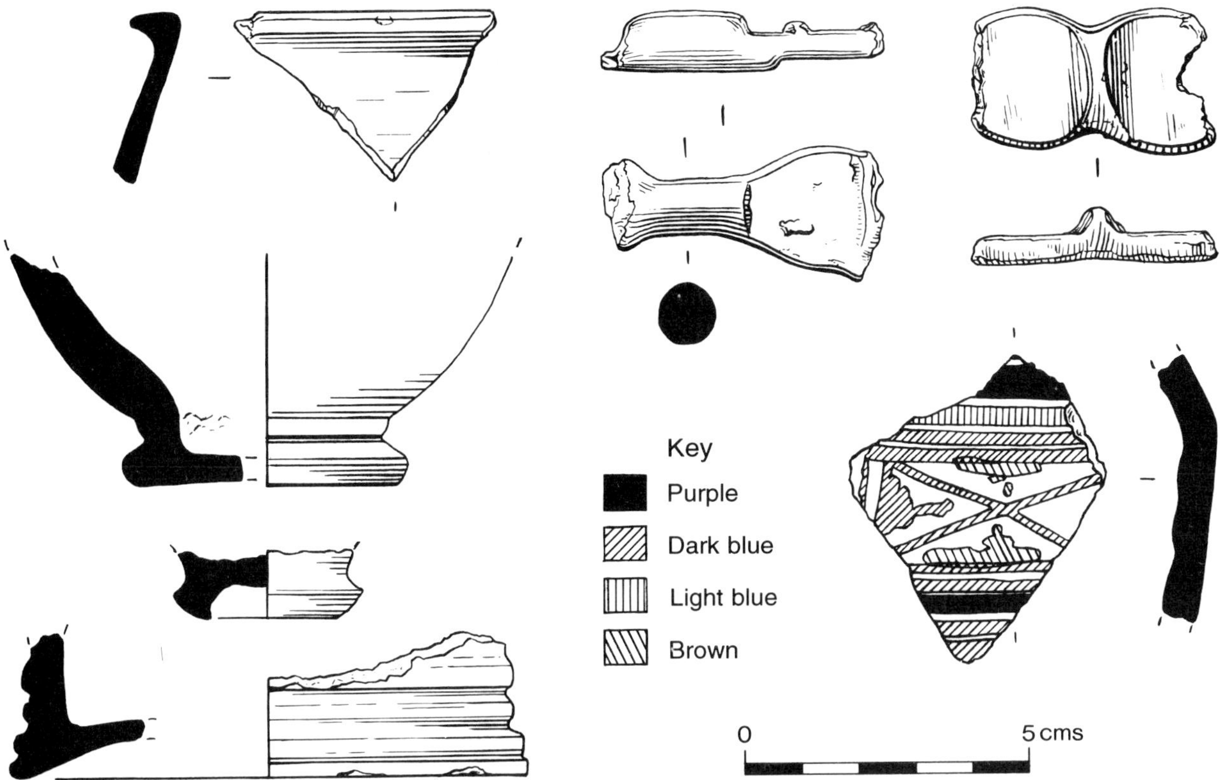

74 *Late sixteenth-century tin-glazed sherds and kiln furniture, probably from the site of the earliest recorded kiln in England on Ber Street (*Karen Guffogg*).*

types, however, might suggest the distinctive cooking habits of an immigrant community; frying pans or skillets seem to have been introduced by Dutch settlers as early as the fifteenth century.

The Strangers were active in other areas besides well as textiles, working as goldsmiths or builders and printers. Two refugees from Antwerp, Jasper Andries and Jacob Jansen, established the first kiln in England for the production of tin-glazed pottery on Ber Street in 1567. This kiln has yet to be located but waster sherds have been found (**74**) and the site is scheduled for redevelopment.

The revitalization of the cloth industry was accompanied by a revolution in the manner of textile production in the city. The medieval cloth trade, although centred on Norwich, was essentially one of rural manufacture and urban cloth finishing and distribution. By the late sixteenth and seventeenth centuries this had changed, with manufacture becoming an important part of the urban process. Much of the cloth was woven by small groups of weavers, working to a master weaver. This meant that production was distributed throughout the city, weavers working in their own homes. The practice was memorably, if perhaps somewhat fancifully, summarized by Daniel Defoe when he visited Norwich in the 1720s:

> if a stranger was only to ride thro' or view the city of Norwich for a day he would have much ... reason to think that it was a town without inhabitants ... the case is this; the inhabitants being all busie at their manufactures, dwell in their garrets at their looms, and in their combing-shops, so they call them, twisting mills, and other workhouses ....

The exaggeration may not be that far from the

mark; twenty years earlier Celia Fiennes had noted that the inhabitants were 'all employ'd in spinning knitting weaveing dying scouring fulling or bleaching their stuffs...'.

Production of cloth certainly did take place in 'garrets' and it is likely that many of the distinctive dormer windows which still grace a great number of Norwich buildings were built to allow light into such workshops. It is apparent from research, however, that such use of garret rooms was only one activity among many. Examination of inventories for the period 1580 to 1730 (some 871 in all) revealed that the percentage of garrets used for working never exceeded 31 (and that as late as 1705–30) while the percentage for sleeping never fell below 53 (1630–54).

Buildings and urban development

This work on inventories complements study of extant buildings and archaeological excavation. The development of houses and house use in post-medieval Norwich is one which has been but little studied. The 1976 Alms Lane site remains the best example of an intensively sampled urban landscape although it is also clear from study of other sites, such as Whitefriars in 1992, that the sixteenth and seventeenth centuries were periods when earlier structures were being divided up to provide accommodation. The inventories, however, many of which relate to parishes north of the river and therefore generally to the middling affluent rather than either to the rich or poor, help chart the development of such features as heated rooms or wash-houses.

The housing situation is of importance because, not withstanding Stranger immigration, the proportion of the East Anglian population living in towns changed significantly during the sixteenth and seventeenth centuries. Population probably grew by half between the 1520s and 1670 but the proportion of the Norfolk population living in Norwich doubled in the same period. The economic and social importance of the city was therefore heightened but the extra people had to have somewhere to live.

It is indicative of the extraordinary size of Norwich and the way in which existing developed land was utilized more rigorously (no doubt encouraged in part by a landlord desire to maximize profits) that the city absorbed the increase in population without significant encroachment on the considerable open space within the walls or by suburban development. The city was indeed notable for its lack of suburbs. Heigham Street, to the west, was a small medieval suburb and an impoverished suburb lay outside the Pockthorpe Gate to the east. This latter was probably established by the sixteenth century.

Aside from these, however, the only suburban development prior to the late eighteenth century was the construction of a manor house on Bracondale at the beginning of the seventeenth century and, in the same location, the building of a Jacobean garden tower from the roof of which were commanding views of the Wensum valley. Both survive. They are of brick, the manor house with characteristically 'Dutch' gables, the tower with brick-mullioned windows and doors.

The later sixteenth century saw a revitalization of public works. Whitefriars Bridge was rebuilt in 1590 while in 1583 John Foster and Alexander Peele, citizens and plumbers of London,

> erected buyled and sette up at or nere New Mylles, a mylle with all things thereto belongeng to dryve and conveighe water by and throughe certaine pypes of lead lyeng and beeyng in dyvers streets and church-yardes to the Market Cross....

A 'systern' was established at the Cross with another on Tombland, although no trace of either has been recorded. Post-medieval water-pipes were observed nearby on St Faith's Lane in 1972 and three intact examples were recovered from excavations on the site of the Greyfriars precinct in 1993.

75 *Gybson's water conduit of 1577 on Westwick Street* (Brian Ayers).

The supply of water was also the function of an ornate conduit erected by Robert Gybson, a wealthy beer brewer, in 1577 (**75**). This stands on Westwick Street (it has recently been re-erected in a reversed position to protect it from traffic) and was built to provide public access to water from a well which previously had been approached via a lane. Gybson was given consent to close the lane provided that 'at his proper costs and charges in a conduit or cock of lead [he] bring the water...up into the street for the ease of the common people...'.

The Civil War and after

Norwich was loyal to Parliament during the Civil War and remote from the fighting. There were alterations, nevertheless, to the urban fabric. The gates to the city were strengthened by rampiring and gun emplacements were established on the castle mound. An arsenal was created in the Committee House; this blew up during a riot in 1648 (the 'Great Blow'), killing many and destroying much glass in St Peter Mancroft Church. The cathedral was desecrated, the evicted Bishop Hall describing the scene:

> What clattering of glasses! What beating down of walls! What tearing up of monuments! What pulling down of seats! What wresting out of iron and brass from the windows and graves! What defacing of arms! What demolishing of curious stonework, that had not any representation in the world, but only the cost of the founder, and skill of the mason!

76 *William Watson's house, St George's Street, with characteristic Norwich dormer windows or 'lucams' restored* (Brian Ayers).

77 *Colegate showing buildings with distinctive dormer windows or 'lucams' (Kirk Laws-Chapman).*

78 *Anonymous painting of 1707 in Anglo-Dutch style housed in Strangers Hall Museum. It depicts Norwich from the east and shows numerous substantial buildings (Norfolk Museums Service).*

The cathedral was spared the fate urged on Parliament by the citizens of Great Yarmouth who petitioned for its destruction so that the materials 'of that vast and altogether useless Cathedral in Norwich' could be used 'towards the building of a work house to employ our most starved poor and repairing our piers...'. Archaeological evidence survives, nevertheless, of the violence done to the building; a piece of lead shot embedded in the monument to Bishop Goldwell is almost certainly a relic of the Civil War. The evicted Bishop Hall went to the suburb of Heigham where his house, now the Dolphin Inn, was bombed in the Second World War, though the restored façade survives.

The seventeenth century increasingly brought greater change to Norwich, even if the Civil War did not. Study of the surviving building stock has shown that many single-celled buildings were erected (such as the house of William Watson on St George's Street (76)

where a single cell unit was attached to a timber-framed building to create a two- or three-cell block) while it is clear from an eighteenth-century painting of the city that it now contained many substantial houses (**78**). The large map of Cleer, published in 1696, does not depict these, showing the built-up areas as blocks of property, but the Corbridge map of 1727 is more detailed, decorating its border with the greater houses of the day.

Many of these were probably built in the traditional timber-framed manner but also utilizing flint and brick, as at 56–60 King Street. These houses, with a flourish of curvilinear gables, are characteristic of many of the now lost seventeenth-century buildings of Norwich.

The growth of population will have led inevitably to social problems such as that of rubbish disposal. Some form of rubbish collection is recorded as early as 1518 and it was noted at Alms Lane that rubbish disposal on site had effectively ceased by the end of the seventeenth century. Quantities of material were certainly being thrown into the river

margins, as evidenced at the Duke's Palace site, to level the riparian land. Such levelling has also been observed on the lower parts of the Greyfriars site, in excavations in the Lower Close and at the castle where vast amounts of rubbish were used to fill the great ditches.

Such movement of large quantities of refuse is likely to have been common; there is a growing body of evidence to suggest that much of the 'hilliness' of Norwich was levelled out by the eighteenth century. The cockeys or streams which were utilized for much of the medieval period tend to disappear from the records although some, such as the Great Cockey, are known to have been culverted. The small stream valleys also disappeared, as observed on St George's Street in 1986 or at the Royal Arcade in 1988 (**80**). Both these had probably been levelled by infilling in the Middle Ages but the lessening of slopes, such as that from the river up Rose Lane, continued in later centuries.

Trade, industry and society

A further consequence of the increase in population was an increase in the importance of Norwich as a regional centre, particularly as a market. The range of market activities

79 *Drawing by John Kirkpatrick of the Castle Bridge and nearby houses. Kirkpatrick, a superb local historian, was active in the 1720s, leaving invaluable notes and drawings* (Norfolk Museums Service/Norwich Castle Museum).

80 *Excavations within the Royal Arcade during restoration, 1988. The site lay within the infilled valley of the Great Cockey stream* (Kirk Laws-Chapman).

astounded Thomas Baskerville when he visited in 1681:

> ...the chief market-place of this city...vastly full of provisions...where I saw the greatest shambles for butchers' meat I had ever yet seen, and the like also for poultry and dairy meats, which dairy people also bring many quarters of veal with their butter and cheese, and I believe also in their seasons pork and hog-meats...and such kind of people as sell fish...viz. crabs, flounders, mackerel, very cheap, but lobster for sea fish and pike or jack for river fish were dear enough. They asked me for one pike under 2 foot, 2s 6d, and for a pot of pickled oysters they would have a shilling. Here I saw excellent oatmeal which being curiously hulled looked like French barley, with great store of gingerbread and other edible things. And for grain in the corn market...I saw wheat, rye, oats, malt ground and not ground, French wheat, and but little barley, because the season for malting was over....

Much of this trade may also be discernible in the archaeological record although, to date, few well-preserved post-medieval contexts have been sampled for environmental analysis. More tangible evidence for the importance of Norwich, and the high quality and variety of material brought into the city, can be observed in artefacts recovered from excavations or watching briefs. At the Castle Mall site, sixteenth- and seventeenth-century material included a decorated German powder horn (**81**), a Palissy ware dish from south-western France with an enamel depiction of St John the Evangelist, a decorated head dress ornament from the Low Countries, ornate Dutch slipwares and, more prosaically, a German bird whistle.

Excavation of a well in St Stephen's Street in 1976 produced a particularly fine range of imported and local ceramics. The imports, both English and continental and which could be split into four phases spanning the seventeenth

81 *Sixteenth-century powder horn from Germany found at Castle Mall in 1990 (*Hoste Spalding*).*

century, consisted of Weser Slipware, Surrey White Ware, Metropolitan Slipware, Frechen Stoneware, Dutch and English tin-glazed earthenwares, a fragment of Hispano-Moresque Lustre Ware bowl, Italian Marble Ware, Dutch Slipware, Staffordshire Combed Slipware and Westerwald Stoneware. The assemblage was atypical in that it was securely stratified but was typical of the range of material recovered on sites across the city. Occasionally more exotic imports are located, such as a Chinese soapstone seal which was recovered from city ditch.

Exports from Norwich were dominated by textiles; pattern books survive from the early eighteenth century with examples of Norwich worsteds, half-silks and callimancoes carefully inserted into the pages. The textile trade was of supreme importance to post-medieval Norwich. It eclipsed all other economic activity between 1660 and 1730 and was fiercely defended by the city authorities. A Weavers Company was formed in 1650 and this supervised much of the output. Many company seals, which were originally attached to the cloth, have been found, notably in London, the main export market. Among other artefacts, a wooden plaque, over 2m (6ft) high and bearing the weavers' arms, survives in the Bridewell Museum.

By the eighteenth century the textile trade had created a number of affluent merchants who left their mark on the city in the houses which they erected for themselves, some of which still stand. John Patteson built a fine house on Surrey Street. The house now forms offices for the Norwich Union, insurance and

banking being two further developments within the city's economy in the 1700s. The Gurney family, which had acted successfully as yarn merchants, created Gurneys Bank in 1775.

More traditional industries such as leather-working remained important in post-medieval Norwich. Quarrying of the chalk hillsides was probably supplemented with mining for flint. Extensive galleries are now known in parts of Norwich, notably beneath Ber Street, off Rosary Road to the east of the walled city, and beneath the Earlham Road to the west (**82**). These galleries are difficult to date, although it is currently thought unlikely that they precede

83 *Road subsidence on Earlham Road in 1988 due to collapse of disused flint-mining gallery (*Eastern Counties Newspaper*).*

82 *Plan of flint workings off Earlham Road drawn in the nineteenth century when names were given to the various galleries (*Norfolk and Norwich Archaeological Society*).*

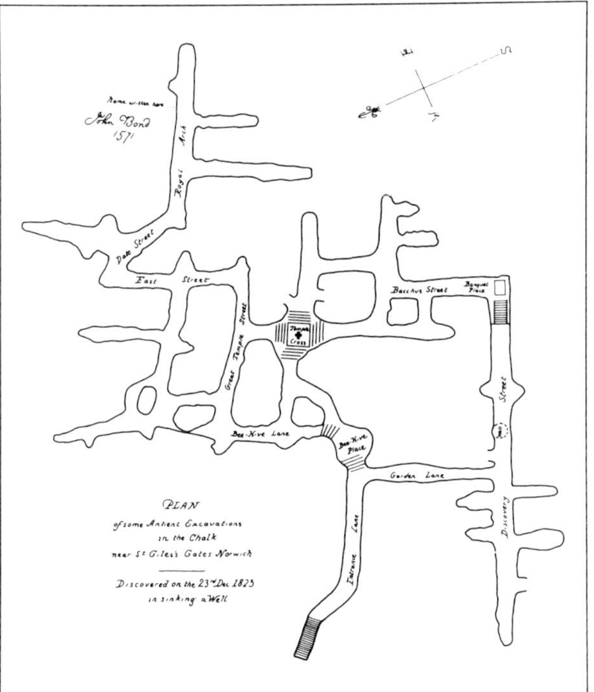

84 *Conservation of early seventeenth-century scriptural text in north aisle of the church of St Martin-at-Palace, 1988. The passage is from the Epistle of St Paul the Apostle to the Colossians, Chapter 3, probably verses 12 to 17. The text does not follow the Authorised Version word for word but was probably painted in 1624 when George Trew was paid 35/- for painting texts (*Kirk Laws-Chapman*).*

the sixteenth century, exploitation continuing into the nineteenth century. Subsidence continues to be a problem when workings collapse. A previously unknown gallery was observed in 1988 after a bus sank into the Earlham Road (**83**). The working was little higher than the seam of flint (some 2ft) with pick marks visible in the chalk.

Other new industries were created, of which an important one for frequent traces in archaeological deposits is that of clay pipemaking. This began in the seventeenth century and fragments of discarded pipekiln have been discovered in post-medieval ditch fills at the castle. Furniture from pipekilns has been recovered from a site on Pottergate, next to the nineteenth-century 'Pipeburners Yard'.

The developing society of Norwich led to a considerable amount of civic building in the later seventeenth and eighteenth centuries. Nonconformity was an important movement in the city and two fine early chapels still stand on Colegate; the Old Meeting House (Congregational) of 1693 and the Octogan Chapel (Presbyterian, now Unitarian) of 1756. The earliest purpose-built mental hospital, the Bethel Hospital, was founded in 1724 and the Assembly Rooms were built in 1754. Both of these structures also survive.

One chapel which does not survive is that of the Quakers, built on part of Gildencroft in 1699. This was bombed in 1942 but the adjacent burial ground, for which licence was gained in 1690, remains.

Public works extended to significant repairs on the city defences in 1727 (primarily the Queen's Road stretch, now entirely lost above ground) and to the levelling of the castle earthworks south of the mound for a cattle market in 1738. This last has recently been investigated in the Castle Mall excavations where it was also clear that systematic exploitation of the castle area for sands and gravels had preceded levelling.

Other public, or at least semi-public, spaces were gardens and orchards. Norwich was famous for these with Corbridge's plan of 1727 detailing many, particularly in the eastern part of the walled city. Much of the Greyfriars site was given over to such gardens and part of a garden and probable path were excavated here in 1993. The Earl of Surrey developed the Augustinian Friary site as gardens and these were visited by Thomas Baskerville in 1681. He arrived by boat where

... the boatman brought us to a fair gar-

85 *Norwich Castle by Samuel and Nathaniel Buck, 1738. This was the year in which the City Corporation determined to level the castle earthworks for a cattle market (*Norfolk Museums Service, Norwich Castle Museum*).*

den ... having handsome stairs leading to the water by which we ascended into the garden and saw a good bowling-green, and many fine walks; the gardener now keeping good liquors and fruits to entertain such as come to see it.

All trace of this garden was destroyed by development in 1970. Smaller private gardens were also worthy of note; John Evelyn wrote of 'the flower-gardens, which all the inhabitants excell in of this Citty...'. Evelyn visited in 1671 and was taken by his host, Sir Thomas Browne, to Browne's famous herb garden which he maintained near the Haymarket in the heart of the city.

Despite the substantial changes wrought by the Reformation in the sixteenth century, the dramatic growth in the wealth of the community in the seventeenth century, and the increasingly diverse economy and enhanced fabric of the eighteenth century, Norwich by the 1780s was still an essentially late medieval settlement in appearance. It was densely occupied but almost the entire population was housed within the walls. The situation is well illustrated by the first detailed and accurate map of the city, that of Hochstetter published in 1789. The date is appropriate; the map depicts the medieval and post-medieval city, an *ancien régime* Norwich, at its zenith. Changes in the 1790s heralded the modern world.

8

The fine city

The antiquity of Norwich was not popular in the late eighteenth century. The greater citizens, worried about the decline in the commercial importance of the city, were anxious to lift some of the burden of inherited medievalism. Agitation was addressed particularly against the city defences with growing calls for their removal. The walls and gates were, in the view of the Norwich Directory of 1783, 'a nuisance, that smells rank in the nose of modern improvement'. Moreover, it was alleged that the existence of the defences inhibited the free movement of air, contributing to unhealthiness in the city. The propaganda was successful and all the city gates were removed between about 1790 and 1810.

The effect, of course, was more symbolic than practical, although the removal of the gates certainly reduced obstruction to traffic. The greatest physical effect was upon the surviving walls, which ceased to be maintained. In places these too were demolished; parts of the stretch at Bull Close Road were toppled inwards to form a platform for house building. Other stretches fell, as happened at Ber Street in 1807. Elsewhere buildings were erected against the wall, either on the interior next to the intramural lanes such as St Martin-at-Oak Wall Lane or on the exterior as at Magpie Road. Other elements were reused: the remains of a cinder oven survive in the western Boom Tower at Carrow.

Suburbs and housing

Development next to the walls obscured the distinctive character of the city and blurred its separation from the countryside. This was exacerbated by the growth of suburbs although these continued to be a slow innovation. Expansion came earliest in the west, with development north of the Newmarket Road outside the city wall at Crooks Place and Union

86 *Houses in The Crescent, an early nineteenth-century development immediately outside the City Wall to the west* (Brian Ayers).

Place by about 1815. This area, South Heigham or the 'New City', was described as having 'handsome rows of houses' in 1846 although conditions were still poor even for the grander type of house such as those on The Crescent (**86**). Here cesspools stood at the backs of houses while buildings in Union Place did not have running water or underground drains.

Very grand planned expansion took place south of the Newmarket Road slightly later in the century with the gradual development of the Town Close estate. The estate had been granted to the mayor, aldermen and citizens by the Cathedral Priory in 1524 and consisted of a triangular area of land of 111 acres (45 hectares), bounded by the Ipswich, Newmarket and Eaton Roads. Used for grazing, it was entered by a five-barred gate, which is depicted on Cleer's map of the city in 1696, although by 1750 part of the area was occupied by Town Close House (now a school). A fashionable suburb was created from 1840 onwards, the City maintaining standards by insisting on high quality workmanship and materials: 'sound Baltic fir, English oak and hard burnt bricks' were all specified, while service roads and sewerage systems were also required.

Houses of the growing middle class were also established to the north of the city. Eleven buildings had been erected on St Clement's Hill between 1824 and 1828. These were handsome structures of brick and slate with appropriate supplements; no fewer than seven of them were furnished with stables. Similarly, about 1830, villas such as The Lawns were built to the east along Thorpe Road while eighteenth-century Georgian development on Bracondale to the south was augmented by large houses such as The Grove.

Elsewhere, the problems of mass housing for an increasing population (68,000 by the time of the first census in 1851) were largely contained within the historic core. While expansion in traditional suburbs such as Heigham took place, much early nineteenth-century housing was provided in the centre. It took two forms:

87 *Sussex Street. Intramural development on part of the medieval Gildencroft (*Brian Ayers*).*

consolidation and extension to existing structures; or planned expansion on areas of open space.

The former, a continuation of a tradition extending back to the sixteenth and seventeenth centuries, led to the full development of the typical Norwich 'court'. Large buildings were subdivided and extended with separate households clustering around a central courtyard. In many areas this led rapidly to insanitary slum conditions. Parts of the city became notorious for the abject poverty of the inhabitants and disease was rife. A cholera epidemic in 1850 led to a government report which established that few houses had a water supply and those that did drew water straight from the river; cesspools were in common use and nightsoil was kept in heaps for sale.

The planned developments were obviously better. An early example was Sussex Street, laid out in 1821–4 across part of the Gildencroft between Oak Street and St Augustine's Street (**87**). Here the houses on the north side form a large terrace of red brick with decorated doorways while, on the south side, there is a terrace of brick two-storey cottages.

Development in the second half of the nineteenth century was predominantly outside the city wall, although terraces were constructed within the historic core in places such as Esdelle Street off St Augustine's Street or Synagogue Street off Mountergate and a grand, if quite 'loose' terrace (to quote Pevsner), was built at the southern end of Surrey Street as late as 1881. Much extramural building took place to the west, off the Dereham, Earlham and Unthank roads. Terraces to the north were not started until the end of the century.

The buildings were of brick, often with the façade being of more fashionable, and more expensive, white brick with red brick at the rear. Roofs were often covered in slate, reflecting the greater availability of materials in the railway age, but traditional pantiles were still used for outhouses and, by the end of the century, were again used on the main house. Sash windows were set in front elevations but, again, traditional casements were frequently retained at the back.

Very many examples of the late nineteenth- and early twentieth-century terraces survive though modernization of windows and doors continues to remove many details. The design of the houses evolved as they were built; early backs had simple lean-to two-storey extensions, while later extensions were gabled. In the early nineteenth century houses were often built two rooms deep with stairs in the rear room. By 1900 a very common plan was for the stairs to rise across the house between rooms. In both cases the buildings lacked a hall, although halled examples were also built.

The expansion of the city can obviously be charted in documentation (many of the plans for terraces survive in the city archives as they were scrutinized by city officials for adequate drainage and other facilities) and in the houses themselves. The disposition of many of the streets and houses, however, owed much to the earlier rural topography and this can also be observed. The triangular nature of the Town Close estate has already been noted, its apex once marked by a gate; similarly, to the north between the Sprowston Road and Magdalen Road, triangular development south of Denmark Road (after the Denmark Farm) is marked at its apex by a large building called Point House. Streets between the Unthank

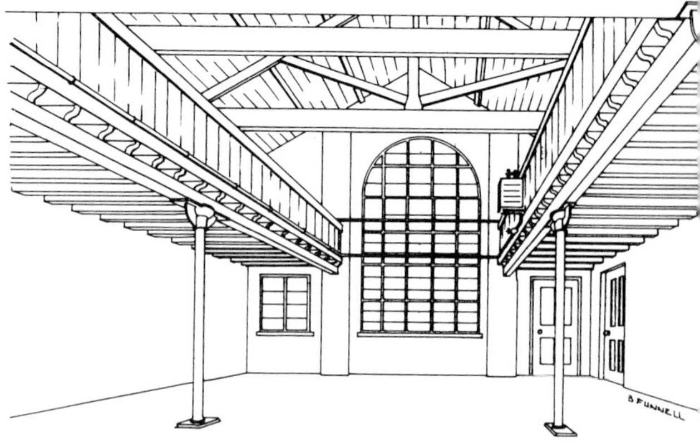

88 *Survey drawing of industrial buildings on Fishergate prior to demolition in 1985 (*B. Funnell, Norfolk Industrial Archaeology Society*).*

and Newmarket roads appear to reflect earlier hedgelines between fields.

Industry

Housing in the nineteenth and early twentieth centuries therefore changed much of the appearance of the city. Within the historic core, the appearance was also altered by the growth of those industries which provided employment for the expanding population (**88**). In many cases traditional activities were maintained. The textile trade continued to be of great importance to the city although it had lost its early eighteenth-century pre-eminence. This was never regained despite valiant attempts to recapture the initiative, most eloquently expressed by the 1836 St James Mill of the Norwich Yarn Company which has been called 'the most noble of all English Industrial Revolution mills' – not an accolade one would expect in Norfolk. The mill was not a success, textile manufacture in 1869 employing only 300 looms, three-fifths of the capacity of the building.

Specialist manufacture of textiles continued throughout the nineteenth century, Norwich being important for the production of silks, crepes and even horse-hair weaving. A crepe manufacturer, one John Sultzer, set up a business next to his house north of Botolph Street about 1820. It is indicative of the amount of open space still available within the walls that he reputedly had a deer park attached to the house as late as 1850!

Leather industries were more successful than the textile trades, however, particularly those manufacturing boots and shoes. Shoemakers had long been a distinctive trade within the city and, by the early nineteenth century, companies of some size were coming into existence. One such was that of James Smith which, after 1816, started to mechanize production in St Peter Mancroft parish (and eventually became the Startrite company). Another was the Norvic company which constructed a purpose-built shoe factory on Colegate in 1856 (this survives, converted to office use). Over 7000 people were employed in the boot and shoe industry of Norwich by 1901 although not all of these were tied to the large firms; there were still more than forty 'garret masters' active in 1910, producing footwear in traditional small, local workshops.

Food and drink were other Norwich trades which blossomed as major concerns in the nineteenth century. Breweries were common (17 were recorded in 1854) with those such as Steward and Patteson or Bullard being of great importance. Bullards built a large brewery on Coslany Street in 1868 with water supplied from an artesian well within the structure; this is now the only major brewery building to survive although it is converted to housing and retail use. The offices of Steward and Patteson's brewery also survive, immediately outside the city wall on Barrack Street, but the rest of the complex was demolished in the 1960s. Brewing continued at Young's Brewery on King Street (where massive expansion in 1970 destroyed the site of the Augustinian Friary) but ceased in the early 1980s. The Norwich tradition of brewing, including a famous 'Norwich Nog' in the eighteenth century, ceased with it.

A mustard works was established at Carrow by the Colman family, occupying the site of Carrow Priory outside the city wall. A house was built adjacent to King Street in the 1850s (now in use as offices) with a spectacular conservatory. The earliest factory buildings to survive date from about 1857; they were positioned next to the river so that the works could benefit from water transport. The complex is still active although mustard is no longer produced in Norwich.

Upstream of Colmans, within the city wall, stands Reads Mill or the Albion Mills. These date from the 1830s, when they were built as yarn mills, but were converted to flour mills in 1932. They supplemented earlier flour mills on Westwick Street, also built in the nineteenth century. Both were located on the river, enabling the use of water transport. Characteristic outshoots for hoists survive on Reads Mill, where sacks could be loaded on and off river wherries. The Westwick Mills were destroyed by enemy action in 1942.

The structural and mechanical engineering firm of Boulton and Paul was another nineteenth-century company which had great impact upon the topography and economy of the city. The firm was important for the production of wire netting (the world's earliest netting machine is now in the Bridewell Museum) as well as sectional buildings such as conservatories and, in later years, aircraft frames (including that of the R101 airship). A factory was originally established off Rose Lane in 1865. This grew to occupy most of the block between Mountergate, King Street and Rose Lane by 1898. Demolition of properties in 1899 revealed timbers of a splendid medieval building which were reused in the company's offices; this survives on Rose Lane as the Tudor Hall and is now a night club.

A further engineering company was that of Barnard Bishop Barnard who had established a large iron foundry north of the river in central Norwich about 1855. Among the products of this firm is the cast iron bridge of 1882 linking Barn Road to St Crispin's Road and which still carries the modern Inner Ring Road. Bridges of iron were a feature of Norwich, the Duke's Palace bridge of 1822 (demolished in 1974 but one span now reused within the Castle Mall development) and Foundry Bridge of the 1870s being other examples. The second oldest surviving river bridge in the city is Sir John Soane's bridge on St George's Street; this has a stone arch and dates from 1783 but it also has a cast iron railing which is probably later.

Urban development

The large industrial complexes located within and adjacent to the historic core had a profound effect upon the traditional topography of the city. Some, such as Colman's, were built on marginal sites, but the acquisition of an area such as the Rose Lane works of Boulton and Paul could only be established by the amalgamation and demolition of many adjacent properties.

In these circumstances it is surprising that streets were not lost as well as many tenement and other boundaries. One street which was

89 *The gasworks at St Martin-at-Palace Plain in 1956. The buildings were demolished in 1970 (©RCHME, Crown copyright).*

closed was that of World's End Lane which ran east of St Martin-at-Palace Plain. A gasworks was constructed north of this street in the 1850s (destroying the medieval town house of Sir Thomas Erpingham); expansion of the works in 1888 removed the lane (**89**). The Colman family succeeded in diverting King Street slightly to the north, thus ensuring that their house would have a carriage drive sheltered from the street. As late as 1920 the Colman company managed to get the line of Carrow Road diverted with the construction of a new swing bridge just inside the Boom Towers. This enabled demolition of the original Carrow Bridge which had carried the road through the middle of the factory site.

New streets were created within the historic centre. A lane connecting the Market Place to the Back of the Inns was established in 1813. This, Davey Place, was named after Alderman Jonathan Davey who had purchased the King's Head Inn (where Parson Woodforde, the eighteenth-century diarist, stayed when he visited Norwich) and pulled it down. Exchange

Street extended north of the Market Place by 1828. Later in the century, the most notable new thoroughfare was made, that of Prince of Wales Road. This was planned as a great sweeping curve from the centre of the city to Thorpe railway station. It was laid out in 1864 and development at the city end was splendid but investment ran out at the lower end of the street and the design was never completed. It is probable that substantial elements of the Franciscan Friary were uncovered during its construction; an unprovenanced plan purporting to show the church may date from this time.

South of the city a road was created up Carrow Hill; this was a philanthropic move by the Colman family, initiated as poor relief. A similar scheme led to the construction of Gurney Road from Barrack Street to the Salhouse Road through Mousehold Heath. The remnants of this heath, which in the sixteenth century had extended some 9 miles (15km) eastward as far as Ranworth, amounted to 184 acres (74 hectares) by 1883 when they were granted by the Dean and Chapter to the citizens of Norwich as a recreational resource.

Communications by road and water were, of course, supplemented by railways in the mid-nineteenth century. The first railway was constructed between Norwich and Yarmouth in 1845, a terminus being provided at Thorpe railway station immediately east of the river Wensum. This station was replaced by the existing station in 1886 but engine sheds of the 1840s survived, the earliest such buildings in East Anglia until regrettable demolition in early 1994. Extension of the railway network led to the creation of two further stations, both also on the edge of the historic core. The City Station was built at Barn Road in 1882; bombed in 1942 it lingered until final demolition in 1960. The Victoria Station of 1849 was situated on Queen's Road. It was demolished and became a coal yard although it is now commemorated in fanciful fake 'ironwork' on the new supermarket which stands on the site.

The physical legacy of nineteenth- and early twentieth-century industrial Norwich is still strong but much has been destroyed. Extraordinary buildings such as the St James Mill do survive, as do structures like the showrooms of Panks engineers on Cattle Market Street, with a splendid cast iron and glass front of the 1860s. Losses, however, while including such important complexes as those of Boulton and Paul on Rose Lane (except the Tudor Hall) and the Barnard Bishop Barnard site, also embrace buildings of less well-known companies. A 1903 cloth factory was standing on Botolph Street as recently as 1962; it was illustrated in the 'Pevsner' guide as a building constructed when 'there was little in England or indeed in Europe quite so functional and unfussy' and exciting a reference to the Glasgow School of Art.

Public buildings

The nineteenth century was also a period when great public buildings were constructed. One of the earliest was the Shirehall of William Wilkins which was built in 1822–3 (**90**), shortly before the construction of his main entrance and perimeter wall to the gaol (now the Castle Museum) of about 1825. The Shirehall was extended in 1906, prompting archaeological observation by E.J. Tench who published a section of the castle mound where the building cut into early deposits. The Norfolk and Norwich Subscription Library was constructed in 1835; it still stands but its books have been transferred to the University of East Anglia. A new fish market was built in 1860; the Guildhall and St Andrew's Hall were both restored and embellished in the 1860s; a Corn Exchange was erected in 1863 (now lamentably demolished); the Agricultural Hall dates from 1882 (currently studios and offices of Anglia Television); and the Technical Institute (now the School of Art) was built in 1899.

Outside the city walls, St Andrew's Hospital was built in 1811–14 as a mental institution, while additions to the Norfolk and Norwich Hospital were made in 1802 and 1879. A city

90 *The Shirehall, Shirehall Plain by William Wilkins, 1822. This building replaced an eighteenth-century structure on the castle mound (itself a rebuilding of an Elizabethan Shirehall). Wilkins' building was replaced by modern Crown Courts in the late 1980s* (Brian Ayers).

gaol was built on Earlham Road in 1827. Military building had started in 1791 with the Cavalry Barracks on Barrack Street. These occupied the site of The Lathes, a grange of the medieval Cathedral priory (subsequently called Blennerhasset House). The barracks in turn were demolished in the early 1970s as was the Drill Hall of 1866 on Chapelfield Road together with a tower of the medieval city wall which had been incorporated into it. The Britannia Barracks of the Norfolk and Norwich Regiment survive, however, on Britannia Road. These date from 1885–7 and retain details such

91 *Causeway bridge piles from Fye Bridge recovered and photographed in 1896* (Norfolk Museums Service, Norwich Castle Museum).

as an integrated sentry box.

Public investment gradually extended to the provision of public services. Street paving initiatives, such as covering Gentleman's Walk in York stone in 1863, were followed by sewage and slum clearance schemes. The first sewers were laid in 1869 and it was the provision of other sewers in 1896 between Elm Hill and Colegate, across the river Wensum, which led to one of the most startling archaeological observations of the nineteenth century, that of a pre-Conquest causeway structure.

Antiquarian study

This causeway was seen and reported by the Reverend William Hudson, one of the greatest of Norwich antiquaries (**91**). He lived at a time when others were also noting the material history of the city, often as a result of observation of a rapidly changing environment. While slum clearance, which was started as early as 1877, did not necessarily attract attention (the antiquarian importance of some of the buildings was probably not appreciated), Hudson, with the likes of F.R. Beecheno and Walter Rye, pursued disparate interests and enthusiasms, laying a basis for much modern archaeological work.

Rye and Beecheno were pioneers of architec-

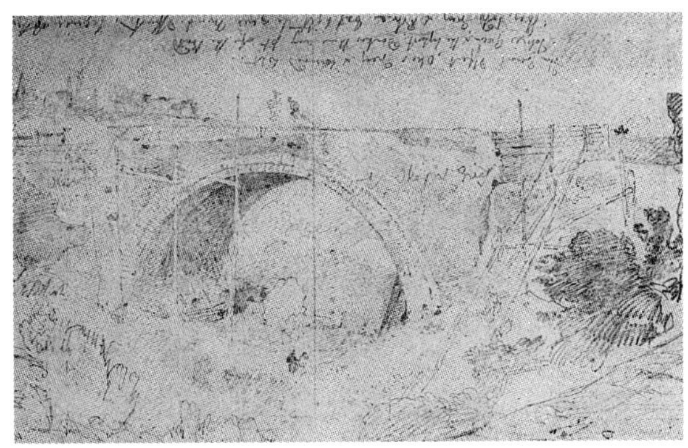

92 *John Sell Cotman – the Castle Bridge under repair in the 1820s (*Norfolk Museums Service, Norwich Castle Museum*).*

tural conservation. Rye might have been scathing about 'the Society for the Prevention of Cruelty to Ancient Buildings' but he also took an active role in preserving ancient structures in the city, purchasing the early twelfth-century Lazar House to save it from demolition. Beecheno too was active in such matters, writing in strong terms to the city council in 1885 to protest at a breach which had been made for a new doorway in the north, flint-knapped and squared, wall of the Bridewell.

The nineteenth-century city was therefore one which, while being modernized, also housed those who cared about its past. Such care was, of course, limited by commercial pressures which remained of paramount importance. George Borrow could write in lyrical terms about the city in 1851 as:

> A fine old city, truly, is that, view it from whatever side you will...perhaps the most curious specimen at present extant of the genuine old English town. Yes, there it spreads...with its venerable houses, its numerous gardens, its thrice twelve churches...a grey old castle...and yonder, rising three hundred feet above the soil...behold that old Norman master-work, that cloud-encircled cathedral spire....

93 *Excavations in Norwich Castle keep in 1889. The man with the sledgehammer is standing on the remains of the Norman spine wall (*Norfolk Museums Service, Norwich Castle Museum*).*

But the 1850s was also the decade which saw the establishment of the gasworks immediately north of the cathedral precinct (it was removed in 1970).

Public utilities and churches

Gas provision was not new in the 1850s; gas pipes were first laid in 1820 and soon afterwards a 'gasolier' had been erected on the Market Place with four gas lamps. Water supply began to improve after a new water works with a filtration system was established at New Mills in mid-century. Municipal cemeteries were provided, firstly at Rosary Road about 1819, the earliest in the country, and then off Earlham Road in 1865. Both retain tombs and tombstones of ornate Victorian design. Late in the century schools were built, such as the Angel Road Boys School of 1895.

94 *Public urinal, Station Road – reputedly the oldest concrete urinal in the world (*Brian Ayers*).*

Public conveniences, male only at first, were built on Tombland in 1878. Others followed at sites such as the forecourt of St Andrew's Hall. A 'Clochemerle' style urinal was established by the early twentieth century in the middle of the north end of Tombland; it was removed in 1919 to be replaced by a pedestal bust of Edith Cavell. Of greatest importance was the positioning of a urinal on Station Road (now St Crispin's Road). This survives, the earliest concrete urinal in the world (**94**).

Increasing care of the physical wellbeing of the population was matched by provision for the spirit. The ancient city remained well-endowed with churches (too well-endowed: the church of St Peter Southgate was allowed to fall into ruins in 1887, the first loss of a medieval church since the sixteenth century; a fragment of the tower arch survives) but new churches were needed in the growing suburbs. The earliest was that of Christ Church, New Catton, built in 1841–2. It was followed by St Mark, Hall Road (1844); St Matthew, Rosary Road (1851); Holy Trinity, Essex Street (1860–1); St Philip, Heigham Road (1871); Christ Church, Church Avenue (1874) and St Thomas, Earlham Road (1886). This last was badly damaged in the Second World War and rebuilt while St Philip was demolished in the 1970s; the others survive.

The greatest church to be built in the nineteenth century, however, was that of St John, Earlham Road (**95**). This was paid for by the Duke of Norfolk and constructed to designs of George Gilbert Scott and John Oldrid Scott as a church for the Roman Catholic community. Fittingly it is now designated as the cathedral church of the East Anglian diocese; the structure is an enormous building in Early English revival style with a length of 85m (275ft).

Chapels were also built, some of them exceptionally large. The Congregational church on Princes Street is a good example, a yellow brick building of 1869 in the classical style. This remains in use, as does the Friends Meeting House of 1826 on Upper Goat Lane and the

95 *St John the Baptist, Earlham Road, built between 1888 and 1910 and now the Cathedral Church of the Roman Catholic diocese of East Anglia (*Brian Ayers*).*

Methodist chapel on Chapelfield Road. Others also survive, often adapted for reuse such as the former Catholic chapel of 1827 on Willow Lane. Others still have been demolished, losses including the 1810 Methodist church on Calvert Street, the 1811 Baptist chapel on Colegate or the Wesleyan chapel of 1858 in Ber Street.

Commercial buildings

Commercial development in the late nineteenth century continued to provide Norwich with some of its finest Victorian buildings. The old post office at the top of Prince of Wales Road, originally built as a bank in 1886, is now part of Anglia Television. A dramatic building faced in limestone with a portico of Ionic columns, it stands opposite the Royal Hotel, built by Edward Boardman in 1896–7 with turrets and ornate decorated brickwork. Another local architect, George Skipper, created the Royal Arcade in 1899 as a tremendous Arts and Crafts structure.

Skipper's work continued into the twentieth century when he was commissioned to design the headquarters building of the Norwich Union in 1903–4 (**96**). This sumptuous structure, with its great marble hall, replaced Surrey House which had been built about 1540. He also designed the ornate Jarrolds shop of 1903–5 and Telephone House in St Giles Street in 1906, a flamboyant Edwardian baroque building.

Norwich, on the eve of the First World War, was thus a typical provincial city with a diverse economic base. It still suffered from overcrowding and slum conditions in the city centre but these began to be addressed as soon as the war was over. A council estate at Mile Cross, the first such in the country, was built between 1918–23 as a civic initiative. From 1924 central government funds were available for slum clearance and rehousing. Expansion of the city gathered pace, particularly to the north, west and east.

Between the wars

The growth of new estates took over farmland, the old farmhouses and cottages frequently surviving among the interwar developments.

96 *Norwich Union headquarters, Surrey Street by George Skipper (*Brian Ayers*).*

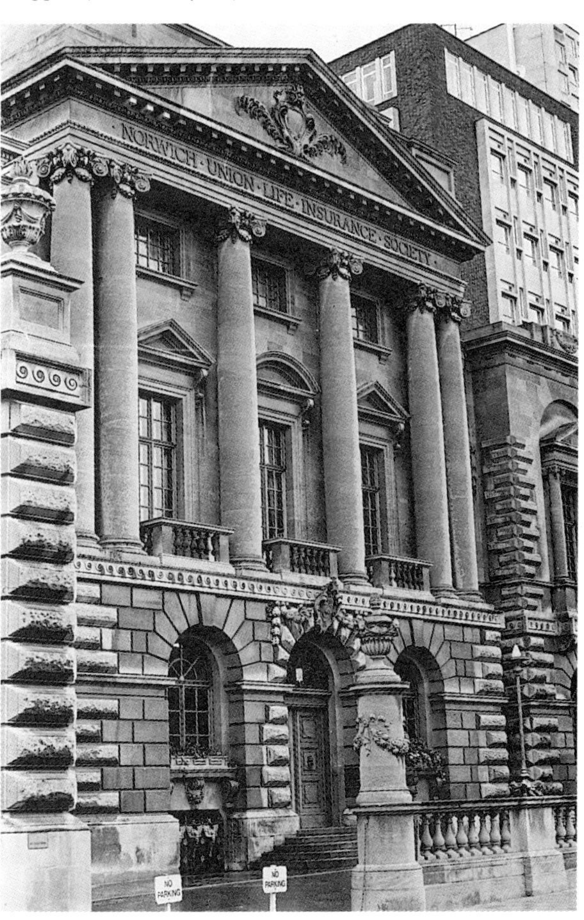

Examples exist on Wroxham Road and Wood-cock Road. City centre development continued as well, the greatest development of all being that of the City Hall which was completed in 1938. This majestic brick building, 'the fore-most English public building of between the wars', dominates a refurbished market place and replaced late nineteenth-century municipal buildings and the medieval Guildhall (the latter being retained).

Construction of the City Hall entailed demolition of considerable numbers of earlier buildings, as did the continuing programme of slum clearance. While the social benefits were clearly great, the archaeological and architectural loss was also significant. The absence of any detailed examination of such structures before clearance meant that the demolition of hundreds of individual properties resulted in the loss not only of fine buildings but also of enormous quantities of information on the social and economic development of the city.

There were those who recognized that the price being paid for modernizing the city was too high. Objectors in the 1930s successfully prevented the destruction of St Stephen's Street, notably the Boar's Head, a celebrated tavern, while Elm Hill, now the city's most famous street, was saved from redevelopment as an industrial estate by the casting vote of the mayor.

97 *Seeking an unexploded bomb at Norwich Cathedral during the Second World War (provenance unknown).*

98 *The fifteenth-century New Star Inn on Quayside prior to demolition (George Plunkett).*

The Second World War

Destruction was accelerated, however, by the Second World War. The city was subjected to 'Baedeker' raids in April 1942 which left much of the south-western part of the historic core in ruins. By the end of the war, bombing had destroyed the medieval churches of St Benedict, St Michael-at-Thorn, St Paul and St Julian (the last rebuilt post-war) as well as the remains of St Bartholomew and the suburban medieval church of St Bartholomew, Heigham.

The south transept of the Cathedral Church was hit by incendiaries, St Stephen's Street was devastated (including, ironically, the Boar's Head Inn), the Midland and Great Northern City Station was badly damaged and late medieval and post-medieval houses were wrecked across the city. Even today an unexploded bomb lies buried close to the north transept of the cathedral; it fell into a well and efforts to dig it out were unavailing (**97**).

The end of the war led to reconstruction and, as in many other British cities, to a paradoxical extension of the attack upon the historic environment, an attack that continued with little official regard for recording or conservation until the 1970s. Losses include the whole of St Stephen's Street, a long stretch of the city wall up Grape's Hill (including two towers and, possibly, the buried remains of St Giles Gate), Stump Cross and much of Botolph Street, the site of the Augustinian Friary, the site (and probably some buildings) of the Cloth Seld (the medieval cloth hall), the galleried White Swan Inn together with its vaulted undercrofts, and the New Star Inn on Quayside (**98**). This last, demolished in 1963, was condemned by one councillor, in a statement which may be apocryphal but which has the ring of truth, as it was known to have been used as a brothel at some time in the past and 'we don't

99 *Bank of Scotland, 1988 by Lambert Scott and Innes* (Brian Ayers).

want buildings like that in the city, do we?'.

To balance these losses, the city has been enhanced by a number of developments. Within the historic core bold buildings have been erected for the Central Library (1962), Eastern Counties Newspapers (1970), Anglia Television (1980), the Bank of Scotland (1988) (**99**) and the Castle Mall shopping centre (1993) amongst others. Within the area of the greater city notable structures have been built at the University of East Anglia (by Denys Lasdun) together with the Sainsbury Centre (by Norman Foster).

One of the more visible legacies of the post-war period in the historic core, however, is not so much new building, which frequently enhances the city, but the way in which the ancient topography was distorted in the years

up to about 1975. Streets, for example, were widened where possible. This has resulted in continuing absurdities, such as Pottergate, where a great and narrow medieval street is interrupted at one point by a modern suite of shops set back from the frontage (**100**). The shops themselves would probably escape much notice if aligned with everything else; as it is, attention is drawn to them, not necessarily favourably.

The lesson to be drawn from the modern development of the city is that the continued and necessary transformation of Norwich works best in concert with the inherited environment rather than against it. Appreciating this lesson has required a new image of the city. 'Historic Norwich' as a concept needed to embrace the entire city, not just the obviously antique. Gradually, in the post-war period, there grew an increasing awareness of the need for more detailed study and care of the city and this came to include buried archaeological deposits as well as standing buildings.

Archaeology since 1945

Post-war archaeological work began in 1946 with excavations conducted by Martyn Jope on behalf of the Norfolk and Norwich Archaeological Society. Further work was undertaken in the 1950s and 1960s by John Hurst, Rainbird Clarke and Barbara Green, but it was only in 1971 that an archaeological unit was established, the Norwich Survey, which allowed a co-ordinated approach involving the study of buildings, documents and archaeology.

Work since 1979 by the Norfolk Archaeological Unit has sought to continue this approach, employing new techniques as they are developed. Archaeological activity in the city is now much more common, in itself forming part of the history of Norwich. It would be churlish, also, to ignore the many other contributions to a greater understanding of the development of the city and its society which have taken place in the modern period. Studies as disparate as those of church bells and ledger slabs, Norwich as a centre of eighteenth-century dissent or even the contribution of Norwich to the history of the telephone exchange have been undertaken, all contributing to an understanding of the growth of the city.

It is therefore necessary, at the end of a work devoted to an appraisal of the development of a great provincial city, to summarize the results of archaeological work and interpretation of the last forty-five years.

There is now a much clearer understanding of the origins of the city although, for the period prior to the eleventh century, the view is still seen through a glass, darkly. Archaeology is at its most 'pure' here, unencumbered by

100 *Modern shops on Pottergate set back from the traditional building line* (Brian Ayers).

historical baggage other than that known for the general region.

Considerable light is being shed on the late Saxon and Saxo-Norman periods when Norwich rapidly gained pre-eminence among the towns of East Anglia. The society, economy and commerce of the settlement is being explored and is complemented by startling discoveries such as a late Saxon timber church, Saxon houses or the well-preserved Norman building.

For the medieval period, the integrated approach of documents, buildings and excavation is enabling a much more detailed understanding of the social structure of the city and of the institutions and buildings which supported it. Study of the urban population is being enhanced by a greater awareness of economic conditions as well as by detailed demographic analysis, particularly of skeletal groups.

This integrated approach is also of exceptional use for the post-medieval period, although here work has not been as intensive as that for earlier centuries. Nevertheless, understanding of the urban fabric, local industry and social conditions has increased dramatically in the last twenty years.

The summary of nineteenth- and twentieth-century development in this chapter has not been able to draw upon much archaeological research, but valid arguments can be made for extending archaeological recording and analysis into the modern period. The city was clearly a place of profound social change in the years up to 1914, with exceptional physical changes in the years thereafter. Limited work to date has demonstrated that much can be learnt of this period from the study of the surviving archaeology, particularly the archaeology of topography and buildings.

Overall, archaeological work has yielded much information about the pre-urban and urban environment and the changes to that environment wrought by people through time. It has defined areas of occupation, isolated hidden aspects of topography and identified processes of change. It is providing information on the daily concerns of the population of Norwich in the past – food, shelter and employment. It is exploring the church and the great urban institutions, lay as well as ecclesiastic. It is helping to increase understanding of trade, commercial and cultural contacts across northern Europe.

Future archaeological work in the city will inevitably be dictated, at least in part, by development pressure. It can, nevertheless, be driven by research goals. These will obviously seek to enhance many of the discoveries listed above and to clarify further the overall development of the city. It is particularly important, however, that evidence is sought to explain the success of the city in its region and its importance nationally.

Perhaps the greatest contribution of archaeology to Norwich, however, is that it encourages a perception of the city as a single entity, one changing continuously but possessing a present integrated with the past. This recognition allows future planning to be undertaken as part of the historic environment. Archaeology is the study of change. The physical shape of the city is the product of such change in the past; archaeological research is the beneficiary of such change in the present; its gift is an understanding of the processes of change to the future.

Chronological summary

Summary table of events

c. 720	Establishment of small villages on both banks of river Wensum	1266	The 'Disinherited' raid Norwich
c. 850	Probable dominance of one settlement – *Northwic*	*c.* 1280–1340	Construction of the city wall
		1349	Black Death
c. 870–917	Probable Danish occupation; construction of defensive earthwork on north bank	1398/9	Cow Tower built
		1404	Charter creates offices of mayor and aldermen
917	Re-conquest of East Anglia by Edward the Elder	1410	Guildhall under construction
	Probable use of Norwich as administrative entre	1430	City water mills built
		15th century	Considerable rebuilding of churches
924–939	Reign of Aethelstan. Coins minted in Norwich	1507	Disastrous fires
		1536–1539	Dissolution of the monasteries
c. 980	First documentary reference to Norwich (in *Liber Eliensis*)	1549	City besieged during Kett's Rebellion
1004	Norwich sacked by the Danes	1565 onward	Settling of 'Strangers' in Norwich
1066	Entry in Domesday Book (1086) suggests Norwich had at least 25 churches as well as 1,320 burgesses	1578	Visit of Elizabeth I
		1648	Civil War riot
		c. 1660– *c.* 1730	'Second City' of England in terms of wealth
1068–75	Establishment of castle and 'French Borough'	1790–1810	Demolition of the city gates
1075	Siege of Norwich Castle	19th century	Development of printing, leather, food industries
1086	Domesday Book entry; number of burgesses fallen to 650	1930s	Slum clearance
		1942	'Baedeker' air raids
1094	Establishment of the cathedral	1945	City of Norwich Plan
c. 1120	Expansion south along King Street	1948	First post-war archaeological excavation
c. 1140	Expansion north-east of the river	1950s/1960s	Excavations by Norfolk Research Committee
1174	Sack of Norwich by Flemings		
1216	Castle falls to Louis, Dauphin of France	1971–1978	Excavations by the Norwich Survey
1226	Establishment of first Friary (Franciscans)	1979–	Excavations by the Norfolk Archaeological Unit

Further reading

Norwich lacks a thorough and up-to-date history of the city. Good introductions are given in Barbara Green and Rachel Young, *Norwich: the growth of a city*, (Norwich, revised edition 1981) or in James Campbell's essay in the *Historic Towns* series: 'Norwich' in M. D. Lobel (ed.) *Historic Towns II* (London 1975). The most comprehensive survey remains that of Francis Blomefield, originally published in the eighteenth century but most commonly available in the 1806 edition of his *An Essay towards a Topographical History of the County of Norfolk, continued by Parkin*, Vols. III and IV (Norwich).

Other early works of great importance for an understanding of the topographical growth of Norwich are those of John Kirkpatrick, especially *The Streets and Lanes of Norwich: a memoir*, edited by W. H. Hudson (Norwich 1889). Hudson himself was a great contributor to the study of Norwich, editing (with J. C. Tingey) a two-volume edition of *The Records of the City of Norwich* (Norwich 1906 and 1910).

There are numerous works on aspects of Norwich although the most influential for the pre-Conquest period is a journal paper: Alan Carter, 'The Anglo-Saxon Origins of Norwich: the problems and approaches' (*Anglo-Saxon England* 7, 1978, 175–204). The Domesday Book entry for Norwich is now available in both transcription and translation: P. Brown (ed.), *Domesday Book: Norfolk* (Chichester 1984) and the volume concerning place-names within the walls has recently been published: K.I.

Sandred and B. Lindstrom, 'Place-Names of the City of Norwich', *The Place-Names of Norfolk*, Part 1 (English Place-Name Society 1989).

A great deal has been written on the architecture, archaeology, artefacts and documentation of medieval Norwich but an overall survey is lacking. Important books which deal with specific topics but which have a national interest are V. D. Lipman, *The Jews of Medieval Norwich* (London 1967) and N.P. Tanner, *The Church in Late Medieval Norwich 1370–1532* (Toronto 1984). A survey of *Tudor and Stuart Norwich* by John Pound was published in 1988 (Chichester).

Reports concerning the archaeology of the city are largely available as academic monographs, papers in local or national journals, or as slim, popular publications. Many have been drawn upon for this work, too many to acknowledge individually here. The most common source is *Norfolk Archaeology*, the journal of the Norfolk and Norwich Archaeological Society, which has published papers on the history and archaeology of Norwich since 1846. The seven parts issued 1972–8 contain interim reports of the work of the Norwich Survey.

The principal publication route for most excavations in the city undertaken in the last twenty years, however, is the journal series *East Anglian Archaeology* (volumes 13, 15, 17, 26, 28, 37 and 58 to date). Recently, popular publications have been issued concerning work by the Norwich Survey (M.W. Atkin and S.

Margeson, *Life on a Medieval Street*, Norwich 1985) and the Norfolk Archaeological Unit (B.S. Ayers, *Digging under the Doorstep*, Norwich 1983; B.S. Ayers, *Digging Deeper*, Norwich 1987; and B.S. Ayers, J. Bown and J. Reeve, *Digging Ditches*, Norwich 1992).

Individual monuments have been the subject of a number of volumes. The cathedral has naturally received most attention and two works amongst many can be mentioned: the publication of John Adey Repton's survey of *c.* 1800 (*Norwich Cathedral at the end of the eighteenth century*, Farnborough 1965) and Eric Fernie's recent publication *An Architectural History of Norwich Cathedral* (Oxford 1993). The castle is less well-known, although recent work on the keep is being prepared for publication as is the report on the massive excavations which took place in and around the south bailey in 1989–91. The volume entitled *North-East Norfolk and Norwich* by Nikolaus Pevsner in the Buildings of England series (Harmondsworth 1962), although outdated, remains a valuable guide.

The best approach to the variety of publications concerning the city, however, is probably through the Norfolk Bibliography. Two volumes of *A Bibliography of Norfolk History* have now been published (Norwich 1975, compiled and edited by E. Darroch and B. Taylor; and Norwich 1991 compiled and edited by B. Taylor).

Glossary

Ambulatory   Semicircular aisle enclosing an apse (*qv*).

Anaerobic   Soil condition where the soil is deprived of air (usually by waterlogging), thus inhibiting organic decay.

Apse   Vaulted semicircular end of a chancel or chapel.

Ashlar   Masonry of large faced and squared blocks.

Axonometric   An orthographic projection in which the lines are to scale length and are inclined in relation to picture plain.

Barbican   Outwork defending the entrance to a castle.

Barrow   Burial mound, usually prehistoric in date.

Borre style   Scandinavian decorative style named after discoveries at a burial site at Borre in Vestfold, Norway.

Chamfered   Surface of a stone block created by cutting across the square angled.

Clerestory   Upper storey of the walls of a church pierced by windows.

Colonnette   Small column.

Conduit   Artificial channel or pipe conveying water.

Corbel   Block of stone projecting from a wall to support a feature above.

Culvert   Tunnelled or buried channel to convey water.

Henge   Prehistoric circular ritual monument delimited by a ditch.

Insulae   Blocks of buildings, usually in a Roman town.

Jamb   Straight side of an archway, door or window.

Leet Court   Local court; Norwich was divided into four administrative areas or *leets*.

Long-and-short work   Saxon quoins (*qv*) consisting of stones placed with the long sides alternately upright and horizontal.

Majolica   Fine Italian pottery coated with opaque enamel.

Moot   Assembly, often a legal court.

Motte and bailey   Norman fortification consisting of an earthen mound (the motte) placed within or to one side of an enclosure (the bailey), both defended by a ditch.

Numismatics   Study of coins.

Pleistocene   Geological period corresponding with the last or Great Ice Age (between 10,000 and 500,000 years ago).

Quern   A hand mill for the grinding of flour.

Quoin   Dressed stone at the angle of a building.

Reredorter   Monastic privy or latrine.

Ring-ditch   Ploughed-out barrow (*qv*) where the infilled ditch survives and can be photographed from the air.

Sherd   Fragment of pottery.

Skillet   Cooking utensil for stews or boiling meat.

Slype   Covered way or passage; in a monastery that between the transept of the church and the chapter house.

Spandrel   Triangular surface between an arch and the mouldings enclosing it.

Topography   Delineation and description of a locality.

Voussoir   Wedge-shaped stone used to construct an arch.

Wattle and daub   Interwoven twigs plastered with clay or mud to form a walling material; late medieval and post-medieval buildings in Norwich had lath and daub infill.

Index

Grid references in squared brackets after street-names refer to illustrations on pp 14–15. Churches and religious houses are located on the same pages.

126